Revealing
The Secrets of
The Game

Exposing the Most Heavily Guarded System of Self-Empowerment Ever Designed

By W. James Dennis

NOTE OF WARNING

The information presented in this book is for reference purposes only. The author and publisher do not in any way endorse nor condone any illegal activity, malicious or vicious acts against another person that may be depicted in the following pages. Therefore, the author and the publisher disclaim any liability and assume no responsibility for the use or misuses of the information herein.

REVEALING THE SECRETS OF THE GAME
Exposing the Most Heavily Guarded System of Self-Empowerment Ever Designed

First Edition

ISBN – 978-0-9915587-4-2 (ebk)
ISBN – 978-0-9915587-5-9 (sc)

TABLE OF CONTENTS

WHAT YOU NEED TO KNOW
PLEASE READ THIS FIRST!

I must make a few points before you go **any** further in this book.

(1) As you read through this book you will see terms like "Player" and the "Game" and other "street" terms used to convey this knowledge. These are the terms I was taught as I learned the Game and I honestly find it easiest to teach it to people this way. **The terms are not important!** Completely disregard them if you wish. The information *is* what's important.

(2) Learning the Game can be exhilarating, but it comes at a price. The information in this book, if you honestly apply it, will cause you to "die" to yourself. The "you", you think "you" are now, will be pulled up by the root like an obnoxious weed in a beautiful garden. You will "die" and be reborn into a more powerful version of yourself. Without trying to sound over-dramatic I must tell you the brutal truth.

You may not realize this, but the "you", you are right now is not the true *you*. Your perceptions on life and pieces of your personality originated from someone or someplace else. The "you", you are now is nothing but a melting pot of other people's opinions and personality traits that you've picked up over the years.

(3) The Game is hundreds of years old. Of course it wasn't called "The Game" back then, but this knowledge had been passed down from mouth to ear through the centuries. Its original intent (as it was told to me) was to empower the lower class so that they would be able to operate with the

same knowledge (or greater knowledge) as their rulers. This allowed them to break-free and rule themselves.

(4) This book **IS NOT** for everyone. Only, maybe one out of 20 people who read this book will be able to receive the full benefit of it. The Game must already be *in* you. If it is, as you read this book it will *move* you. This information will stir something inside of you and you will find yourself feeling as though, somewhere deep within yourself, you already "know" these things. The Uncommon Sense will make perfect sense.

(5) This information is not evil or malicious in intent. The Game has been used this way in the past and still is today, but that was not its original intent. I also must mention I am not a "New-Age" guru, spiritual teacher or a member of some mystery cult. I am a Hustler, a realist, exercising certain layers of the Game for financial gains and more freedom in my personal life.

(6) The reason this information is kept hidden from you is because it empowers you. It expands your awareness. When you know the Game, you can no longer be misled or fooled by those who manipulate you through it. When you don't know something, you are a slave to those who do know.

(7) This is very important. You must understand that the Game is not a quick fix for anything. Your life is not going to miraculously change overnight. It will take practice, time, determination and patience. But you have that, right?

A few more things – it is generally accepted that life is the best teacher. If you are very observant you can learn many things just by living day to day. The problem with this statement is that what you learn from life is completely dependent on how aware you are. How your mind filters and translates your life experiences. Our filter is usually not ours but someone else's. It is taught to us through the media, music, movies, family and friends. They tell us what to think, how to think, how to feel, what to feel, what is of value and what is not of value, what is acceptable and what is not acceptable.

As you learn and practice these principles to become skilled at them, you will be reformed – shaped and molded through the trials and tests that will come. It's like a Japanese blacksmith who forges the katana (samurai sword) through intense heat; the metal is destroyed but re-shaped into something powerful and useful. The blade is then polished to make it beautiful. This is very similar to the process of the Game when you begin to live it. To quote an old saying, "When you decide on a course of action in your life, life shows up." There is a reason for this and it will become clearer later on in this book.

There are many Players in the Game that are going to think I am giving away too much information, but when I look at the state of the Game, and the World in general, I know I have to do my part to educate and help bring the Game back to a state of purity.

This book is about the Game itself. When you fully understand the Principles and Lessons contained here, you will excel at whatever "Game" you want to undertake in life. Every other "Game" that exists is built on the foundation of knowledge this book provides. You will understand why certain things work in other "Games" and why certain things don't. Whatever knowledge you gain from other "Games" will make more sense and be crystal clear once you've mastered this book.

You are responsible for the knowledge you have. As you learn the knowledge in this book you will become responsible for it. If you are ready, then continue. If not, I understand, no harm done. You only have *one* chance to walk away from the Game. If you are *not* ready then turn back now.

GAME - The Dictionary Definition

1 - **a :** activity engaged in for diversion or amusement
b : often derisive or mocking jesting

2 - **a :** a procedure or strategy for gaining an end
b : an illegal or shady scheme or maneuver

3 - **a** (1) : a physical or mental competition conducted according to rules with the participants in direct opposition to each other (2) : a division of a larger contest (3) : the number of points necessary to win (4) : points scored in certain card games by a player whose cards count up the highest (5) : the manner of playing in a contest (6) : the set of rules governing a game (7) : a particular aspect or phase of play in a game or sport

CHAPTER ONE
The Outlook – The Structure of the Game

I am often asked, "What is Game?" or "What is *the* Game?" My usual response is, "Game cannot be defined in a sentence or two but if I had to give you something straight forward I would say Game is self-empowerment through Uncommon Sense."

And, what is Uncommon Sense? Well you know how people tell you to, "Think outside of the box"? Well with Uncommon Sense you don't have to think outside of the box because you *live* outside of the box. By the time the average person thinks they may have it wrong, they re-evaluate and attempt to think "outside of the box". By the time this is done, you're already three steps ahead of them.

With that being said, one large part of the Game is reversing the power dynamic – learning to work the system that keeps you powerless so that you gain power. The Game is much deeper than that, but it's the most common way the Game is used.

I was introduced to the Game when I "crossed over" or "put my foot down" (also called "touching down") into being an entrepreneur. Prior to that I had always been fascinated by the mind and the "spiritual" insights of the wise. The men around me that made the biggest impression in my life all held certain qualities. I didn't realize this until I got older, but it turned out to be an eye-opener. The men that made the greatest impressions on me were all disciplined, great thinkers, confident and good at what they did. They were renaissance men.

My entrepreneur role models had a lot of Game, but they could never break down just what the Game was. The concept of the Game is an anomaly; it exists outside of normal description, form or rule. Without sounding like I have my head in the clouds, all I can say is – The Game just "is". It is what *it is*.

The best way to break this down is to use a concept from a popular movie. Think of it like The Force in, <u>Star Wars</u>. The Force has a "light side" and "dark side". The Force just *is* but can change depending on who uses it and for what purpose. There are multiple layers to the Game and many ways to apply it. It is just like fire – you can cook food and warm your home with fire, but you can also use it to burn a home down or even kill.

Every application of the Game will yield a result and the result, whether positive or negative, will come back to the person who initiated the action (in some form or fashion). Many people coin this as, "What goes around comes around," or Karma. In the Bible this is stated as "…for whatever a man sows, this he will also reap." In the Game we call this Justice. Everyone, regardless of stature in life, must reap what they sow. No one can escape this because it is energy, energy cannot be destroyed only changed into a different form (transmuted).

Life works in cycles and rhythms. When you initiate an action, that energy travels from you to its "destination" and then comes back to you, like drawing a circle on a piece of paper. No one knows where the beginning of the circle is except for the person who closed it. Your Justice begins and ends with you. You're the person holding the pencil and drawing the circle.

To fully understand the Game it has to be lived and experienced. You can read this book 20 times and still never come close to reaping the rewards of self-empowerment. For you to begin to understand the Game, it must already be in you. If it was not in you, you would have never come across this book. While this sounds all mystical and magical the simple truth is that your attention would have been somewhere else and this book would have flown under your radar.

This book was attractive to you because there is something in you attracted to this type of information. And where does that attraction come from? It comes from an inner need to improve yourself; to make yourself more than what you are now. Not everyone has those thoughts or desires and that is fine, that is how it is supposed to be. There will always be those that lead and those that follow. The best leaders however, are those that are the best students (not followers).

The Game has been around for centuries in various forms. If you ask the Player (those that use the Game), they will tell you that the Game is god-sent. It is the natural order of things. From predators hunting and killing prey onto heat melting ice, there is always a stronger force that is dominant over a weaker one. But even a weak force, can resist a stronger force. 20 zebras working together can possibly kill a lion, and even the intensity of the sun cannot melt a polar cap over many years. A stronger force becomes weaker when its energy is spread out.

To begin to get a picture of what this Game is about we need to look at strong or dominant forces and weak or submissive forces. Against one another the strong will eventually overtake the weak, but a weak force alone is pretty stable unto itself. Using our heat example, if I am in a cold room and get me a substantial source of heat, the cold will eventually dissipate. But in a cold room with no heat source, the cold is dominant. Now what is the purpose of knowing this you ask? Simple, let's look at the pyramid structure. The structure of the Game.

Pyramids, like those in Egypt and around the world are built with a wide base at their bottom and they get smaller in size as they go up toward their top. The base supports everything above it. If you started taking stones from the base of the pyramid, you would weaken the structure and it would eventually topple over. But if you took just the very top blocks off the pyramid and placed them on the ground, they are still perfectly fine. And the base of the pyramid would still be standing as well.

Now let's look at the Monarchy structure – The King, The Queen and their subjects. The King is the supreme ruler of his lands. The Queen is his wife and it was part of her duty to give birth to a male heir so that the kingdom would stay in the royal blood line. It was the subjects (base of the pyramid) of the King (top of the pyramid) that gave the King power. Just by the fact that his subjects accept his rulership, he has it.

Now, do the subjects need a King to survive? To answer that question you need to understand what a King's duty was. The main purpose of a King was to lead his armies, protect his lands (and the subjects on it) and to dispense justice. To sum all this up, the King was a manager. The King had other duties of course but these were his most important.

So, now that we know that, do the subjects need a King to survive? Can the base of the pyramid exist without anything built on top of it? Of course it can. The subjects could defend their own lands and dispense their own justice. The subjects could exist without a King, but the structure would be incomplete. An incomplete structure is a structure with no purpose, anything without a purpose is useless but anything that is serving a purpose is in a state of order.

Without order (a structure) in place, who could say that this land is mine and not yours, unless we agree where the line is at?

What would I do if I suspect my prize cattle was stolen by someone miles away? I could of course grab my friends and family and go try to bring the thief to justice, but my family and friends would have to agree that I was in the right. What if I am wrong about this alleged thief? Or what if I am lying and secretly want this "thief" dead for a personal reason? Without a set of guidelines and principles there is no order. Human beings have yet to evolve enough to live without a complete structure or a **perceived** complete structure.

Now can the King exist alone without subjects? Of course he can, he would not hold the title King, but he could farm off the land and live an existence just fine.

A King is the highest level manager of a kingdom. To maintain his power he must keep up with his duties. He must deliver. The subjects will grow restless when he doesn't. And despite the King's military might, a well laid plan and the right amount of effort will get a King (who does not deliver) murdered, assassinated or usurped by someone else.

If a King's forces, whether physical or mental, are scattered he is susceptible to losing his power. His power must remain focused and concentrated. This is the King's strength and weakness. A King is always under pressure to deliver and a King has no power outside of his Kingdom. A King cannot leave his Kingdom and enforce his rule where it is not wanted or accepted, he is at that point nothing but another man.

This structure has been in place all throughout human history. From Babylon, to Persia, to Ancient Egypt, to Greece, Rome, feudal Japan all the way up to the modern day. Every major country in the World operates under this same structure. Now you know the real meaning of the phrase, "The names change, but the Game remains the same."

Every corporation across the world runs under the pyramid structure. The few at the top make their living off of the many at the bottom. Is this fair? From the perspective of the Game, yes it is. Why? Because the many at the bottom freely accept it and labor under it.

Why does a professional athlete who makes millions of dollars over their lifetime never become a franchise owner? Why do they become commentators and coaches who teach and speak about the sport they love?

Why does a recording artist attempt to return to the stage after years away? Why do they try to reestablish their careers long after the industry has moved on and the fans have found new artists to worship?

It's not due to lack of money, skill or social connections. Many of these athletes and artists have opportunities to do almost anything they choose – but they don't. The reason is because of the mentality. They are addicted to the Game. Not as a dominant force but a submissive one. Their entire careers are based around upholding someone else's power structure and they never break out of that mold. They long for the recognition above them and the roar of the crowd below them.

The structure of the Game has been ingrained into almost every facet of our society:

You have the King, **CEO/owner** and the Queen, **President and Vice President**.

Next you have the Royal Court, the **managers** or **coaches** who perpetuate the structure. They train the King's subjects about the "Game" and keep them under control.

Then you have the King's subjects (merchants/craftsmen), the **employees**. They are the backbone of the Game; everything is built on top of them and around them. Without them the structure of the Game would crumble.

And finally you have the peasants, the **consumer**. Without the peasant (those who use what the Game produces), there would be no Game. They are the only people who can move in and out of the Game whenever they choose, but they are so dependent on the structure that they rarely leave.

The King is known about, but rarely seen. The King (CEO/owner) stays in his castle and hardly ever mingles with his subjects (employees). He is more a symbol to them than anything else but his authority is hardly ever questioned.

Again you might ask, is this fair? It *is* fair from the perspective of the Game. An owner of a company cannot just get up and leave. If the ship sinks, he has to go down with it, so to speak. An employee on the other hand can take his skills and find another employer at any time. Remember, a King is only a King because his subjects accept him as such. Now you know the real meaning of the phrase, "You can be anything you want as long as one person believes in you."

Viewed through a certain filter, the Game is part psychology and part sociology and yet something more. The Game is a certain kind of knowledge which I call Uncommon Sense. It is that which is kept from you so that you will forever remain a subject in someone else's kingdom. Within this knowledge are a set of principles and these principles form a system. This system, for lack of a better term, is self-empowering. This system allows the subjects of a Kingdom to come together to form their own Kingdom. In sociology this is sometimes called a sub-culture, but it really is just raising yourself up and operating with the same knowledge the King has.

At your job, if you knew as much or more than your boss (in a perfect world) you could easily take their place. With the Game, you can no longer be led or fooled by those in higher positions because you will be mentally operating on the same level as them.

With this knowledge, you will transform from a weak source to a strong source; from submissive to dominant. But always remember this rule of the Game. Even a weak force can overcome a stronger one. Water can cut through a stone if given enough time and/or force. To remain a strong dominant force you must never spread out your energy too thin, meaning trying to do too many things at once (or focusing on too many goals at once). You must choose a purpose, a direction and fully commit.

The Game, if played at the highest level, is not manipulation, deceit or trickery. The Game is brutal truth and uncompromised honesty.

Let's take a step back in history for a brief moment.

As I've already mentioned, the Game has been used throughout history. Every culture had possessed their unique approach to it. They were viewed as mere thieves and criminals by those in power. Many of these "secret" organizations did not start out being involved in criminal activity. Unfortunately though, some did.

Don't worry; I am **NOT** advocating criminal activity in **any** way. I just want you to see what some don't want you to know. Here is just a short historical list of those who used a *small* portion of the Game for the best or the worst.

The historical figure **Robin Hood** used it. Not the Robin Hood you see depicted in cartoons and movies, but the **real** historical figure. He was considered a Yeoman, "a commoner who cultivates his own land". He was the ultimate wolf in sheep's clothing. As the story goes, he used his status and knowledge of the nobility to rob from them and give to the poor. He turned the established power structure against itself. Now, what would possess a man to do this? And where did he come up with the idea?

The *original* Sicilian **Mafia** (Cosa Nostra) used it.

The predecessors to the Japanese **Yakuza** used it. The

Tekiya, Bakuto and the Kabukimono.

The Chinese **Triad** was formed out of it by way of
the **White Lotus Society** (as many believe).

The so-called **Russian Mafia** used it. In fact, they took the
Robin Hood approach – taking from the rich and giving to
the poor.

And finally in **America,** it turned into what is known as
pimping, hustling, macking and now we have pick-up artists.
These "sub-cultures" claim to use the Game but this
was **not** the original intent of this system.

Back in the early days of America the term, hustling,
originally meant to make money. It was a legitimate business
term. Unfortunately this term became synonymous with
conning people. These historical "hustlers" played "con-
games". The so-called "hustler" would pick a "mark"
(victim) and **trick** them into giving up large sums of money
whether through scamming or gambling. And what do
pimps and prostitutes call their customers? They call them
"tricks" – they run mental "con-games" on them. A skilled
prostitute knows how to get every last cent she can out of a
client. This is a subtle form of turning power against
someone who **perceives** they have power. The Game is won
before it even begins.

A seasoned and experienced pimp is the only man that a
prostitute can't "trick". This forces her to be truthful with
him because, Game recognizes Game. You can't use the
Game successfully against someone who knows it.

Again, I am not advocating pimping, prostitution or illegal activities – I just want you to be aware of the Game's many "layers" throughout history.

Let me make this clear before we move forward. The Game is **not** about being a criminal or con-man. The Game is **beyond** hustling. The Game is **beyond** pimping. The Game is **beyond** macking. All those "Games" came from the true *original* Game. And the true *original* Game, which this book will reveal to you, is the foundation which all other Games are built on. The Game is more vast and deeper than you have been led to believe.

The Game was never meant to be criminal. It was never meant to be manipulative or deceitful.

All of these organizations or "sub-cultures" grew out of the need for the lower class to operate in their own system of power. The structure they used is the same structure that *every* system of power uses – the pyramid structure. All these groups had rules, regulations and codes of conduct. Many also had initiations that had to be taken before you were allowed to join.

Unfortunately, what may have started out as something positive and empowering began to change into the extortion and brutalization of the lower class. The very same class of people these organizations grew out of.

Now, the question on your mind should be – how did *all* these people from different lands and cultures, separated by time, come up with similar methods to "free" themselves?

Enough of the history lesson, let's get back to why you are reading this book.

This book is a series of principles. If you "stand on" these principles at all costs you will be on the road to mastering the Game. The Game will be *in* you and life will change around you. Opportunities will open and matters which at one time stressed and worried you will be no longer be of consequence. You will be able to see "through" things when you look at them. The masses will think you are crazy, but you will smile with confidence because you will know that the Game is not for them; not everyone is meant to be a King or Queen.

The reality is, when you know something that someone else doesn't, you immediately have an advantage over that person. This right here is a small form of self-empowerment.

Imagine, two men are lost in the woods. One is your average corporate exec and the other grew up learning to hunt and live off the land. This man that knows how to live off the land has a tremendous advantage over the executive. Our survivalist knows how to get food and water – he knows what plants and berries to eat and what to avoid.

Now if our survivalist was a despicable person, he could tell the exec to eat something that could possibly kill him. Or he could just refuse to help feed him altogether. In this situation, whose knowledge gives the greater advantage?

Before we get into the Game, let's set up the scenario:

It is a cold night in winter; the room is rather small and quiet, but warm. The only light comes from a single soft-white fluorescent bulb from the ceiling fan. The curtains are closed and the rest of the house lays in silence.

The student enters the room and greets me with a strong handshake and a sincere embrace.

I motion for the student to sit down next to me on the comfortable brown sofa in the room. We sit down. My student is a "square", someone who knows the term, "Game" and has "soaked up" (learned) some Game by listening to a few YouTube videos and some hip-hop songs but that is the extent of their knowledge. And from someone *with* Game, that is no knowledge at all.

I asked the student that this session not be recorded but they were allowed to take notes. I explained the best way to learn the Game is through questions and answers, but to really understand the Game, it needs to be practiced and Played. Knowledge comes first, then wisdom (knowing how to use knowledge) and that leads to understanding.

I explained to the student that the Game has many layers and can be applied to many things. We were focused that day on how the Game applies to self-empowerment and winning in life. In my opinion, this is the most important layer to the Game. It makes everything you want to do in life much easier. There were to be seven major principles to discuss. The student would be allowed to ask questions but make no observations, only listen and "soak" the Game up.

I made sure we both had our bottles of water and that both our cell phones were completely turned off. The next couple of hours would be just the student and I face to face and mouth to ear; an intense crash course on the Game. Now that the scenario is set, let's keep it moving.

We're about to get into the first principle of the Game. It is through this principle that all the other principles will make more sense and be more readily understood. It is the most misunderstood aspect of the Game and the one where most people fall short.

CHAPTER TWO
Principle One: Justice

The Principle – *Justice is word for word, action for action and thought for thought. What comes back to the initiator is not just what they've done, but also everything that grows out of what they've done.*

Question: So this principle is basically saying, what goes around comes around?

Answer: Yes it is. But there is a deeper level to that. Everything you do, every word you speak and every thought you think is a real thing. It is energy in motion. Energy cannot be destroyed only changed in form (or rechanneled).

When you do, say or think something, you are starting a cycle. That cycle travels into the world and will eventually end back at its source – the person who originated it. Think of drawing a circle on a piece of paper.

Now while this energy is in motion, it will affect other people and other things. These effects can be positive or negative depending on the initial action, word or thought. Whatever grows out of that initial action, word or thought will also come back to the originator of the cycle. Just like "closing" the circle you were drawing on a piece of paper.

Q: So if I do something bad to someone else, something negative will happen to me? Like, let's say I steal money from someone. Will that money I stole eventually get stolen from me?

A: No the money will not necessarily be stolen from you, but you will have to pay for whatever grew out of that initial act of theft.

Let's just say the money you stole caused the person you stole it from to lose his or her apartment. That was the only money they had and their intention was to pay their rent. You not only violated this person but you also caused them pain and hardship. You will receive the results of not just the theft, but the pain and hardship you caused that person – them losing their apartment.

That money is not yours by right. You did not earn it. You must rightfully earn everything in this life to truly call it yours.

I can give you money of my own free-will and out of the kindness of my heart. That money would be yours. But if you stole that money from me or manipulated me into giving it to you, that money is not rightfully yours. It was not earned in an honest straight-forward way.

Q: So what about having a job? Aren't the owners of those companies getting over on their employees? They make hundreds or thousands of dollars off of me working and they might only pay me twelve dollars an hour. Isn't that a form of stealing?

A: Only if you were tricked or manipulated into that situation. If you knew what the arrangement was upfront and you agreed to it of your own free-will, then no, the Justice they receive will not be anything bad or negative.

It is an upfront agreement between two people or parties. Either person or party had the right to walk away from the agreement or re-negotiate.

Q: I hear the term free-will again. Why is free-will so important?

A: Free will is the power to choose. Human beings have a natural desire to feel as if they are in control of their lives and that is because we have free-will.

Whenever you take away the power of choice from a person, whether through deceit, trickery or manipulation, you are in "Violation the Game". When you violate the Game, you can expect negative results to come back to you. Remember, it is more than just what you did, but everything that grew out of what you did.

To make it easy, whenever you hear the term "Violation of The Game", it means you are setting a cycle in motion that will bring negative results back to you. When you are "Respecting the Game" (or playing the Game properly), you can expect positive results to come back to you. Be good to the Game and the Game will be good to you.

The Game never stops. It is always moving and in motion. It may take a month, six months or even years, but you must eventually pay for *everything* you do in one way or another.

People from the streets already know this to some extent. It is called, "paying dues". They know that you must put effort into something before it will work out for the best. This is Justice in motion (operating). You are acting, thinking and speaking things into existence. You are setting cycles in motion that will eventually come back to you.

To truly possess anything and call it yours, you must earn the right to it. You earn that right through operating within the Game. Setting cycles in motion that will allow you to receive what you want. Not through trickery, deceit, lies and manipulation but through focus, determination and hard-work. You should always respect the Game.

Q: But I see people who are liars and manipulators prosper everyday. They have more than honest people. How does that work?

A: People have free-will, remember? You can do whatever it is you want and however you want at any given time. The reason deceitful people prosper is because they are using the Game. Most good, "honest" people are too afraid to use the Game or even learn it. The Game goes against what they have been taught is right or good. I call this Uncommon Sense for a reason. Many of the things you have been taught were "right" are actually things that make you a submissive (weak) force. You were taught these morals and values so that you can be easily controlled and manipulated by people in power.

Going to the example from the movie, Star Wars and The Force – The Force just *is*. But people can use it for positive or negative means. It is the same thing with the Game. Liars and manipulators prosper because they are using the Game against people who don't have Game. But they are using the "dark side" of it, the negative side. Whatever they earned by using the Game in this way will eventually be taken from them. They will lose it. Justice cannot be stopped, only delayed.

Q: How is Justice delayed then?

A: The most common way is through showing mercy (compassion shown to the person who offended you). When you show mercy to someone that has wronged you, you delay their Justice. There is nothing wrong with showing mercy, this is good for your own personal Justice (if it's sincere), but you should be mindful about who you show mercy to and for what reason.

Be careful! Mercy is one thing, forgiveness is something else entirely. Forgiveness is the act of giving up your resentment and the right of receiving compensation from the offender. When you forgive, you release the offender of their wrong doing, completely. This is why in the American court system they will never forgive you or apologize, but they will show you mercy. It's the Game, and now you know why.

I'll make this clearer. When you forgive someone you take on a part of their Justice. Part of what they were going to receive comes to you instead. Be mindful of who you forgive.

Q: So you are saying Justice is like cause and effect?

A: Everything is cause and effect. That is how nature works. Everything has an effect on something else. You cannot get healthy and lose weight by eating foods that make you fat. You will not meet the man of your dreams if you never leave the house. You cannot make money if you have nothing of value to sell. And you cannot progress in life until you stop doing those things that keep you in the same place – the state of mental and emotional bondage.

You must earn everything you get in this life. Justice will ensure that you will receive what you earn.

Q: So through using the principle of Justice I can have a better life?

A: Not through the principle of Justice alone. But when you fully understand Justice, you can begin to predict results. You know that if you are not doing anything to improve your life, then you will get nothing in return. The cycle of doing nothing, returns nothing. It's so simple that people forget it.

When you hear the phrase, "The Game is to be sold and not told," People see the word "sold" and immediately think money. That is not what that means (in most aspects of the Game). One of the meanings of that phrase is that you must "pay" through your blood, sweat and tears to earn the right to *have* Game and be *in* the Game. You have to be tested and what you receive through Justice will be your tests. Every "Violation of the Game" you make has consequences. But as you're mastering the Game you will learn to make fewer and fewer mistakes. You must prepare for the consequences of what you do. Everything has its price and you must be willing to pay it.

To better understand "Paying the Price", look at it like this. To start a fire you need something that is flammable, something to make a spark, oxygen, etc. If you are missing any of these components, then guess what? You will not create a fire (I am not talking about chemical fires). This is the same thing with the Game, you need all the parts in place to get to empowerment. Acquiring these parts and putting them together is part of the price that must be paid. Remember, you must earn the right to have things and doing nothing, returns nothing.

CHAPTER THREE
Principle Two: Purpose

The Principle – *The cause you choose must be higher than yourself. A purpose is the end destination of a journey. You must always know where you are headed or you will never get there.*

Question: When you talk about having a purpose, are you talking about having a goal?

Answer: No, goals and purpose are two different things. Goals will lead you to your purpose. You will have many goals, but there should only be one purpose. Goals change because you as an individual grow and change as you learn new things. A true purpose rarely changes, and it may take a lifetime to achieve a purpose.

Goals are the individual letters of the alphabet. A, B, C, and so on. A true purpose is the *whole* alphabet itself. It is composed of **all** 26 letters and they all must be there. If all the letters are not there, the rest of the alphabet is not complete and therefore serves no purpose.

Q: So if a purpose is made up of goals, what is purpose exactly?

A: When someone is drowning and their very life is at stake, their goal would be to survive long enough to either swim as close to safety as possible or scream for help. The purpose of these actions is greater than their goal(s). Their purpose at this very point is survival, plain and simple. They are focused, nothing else matters at that point. They are not thinking about their house, money, all their clothes and possessions. They are thinking of living and probably seeing their loved ones again. Their purpose is higher than their goals; to continue living. And how do they continue living (achieving their purpose)? By achieving the goal of getting help or getting to safety.

Let me clarify this by giving a couple of analogies. A purpose is like eating to nourish the body. Cooking and prepare the food is the goal. A purpose is like raising a healthy, intelligent well-rounded child. Spending time, showing love and instructing them are the goals.

Going back to the structure of the Game – the purpose is the strong or dominant force. Goals are the submissive force. All goals should feed and fall in line with the purpose.

Q: So what is my purpose, or how do I find one?

A: This comes through the process of what is called negation. That is thinking about everything that is *not*.

Now that you know a purpose is something greater than yourself you can negate goals in your life and define your purpose.

Being wealthy or rich is a goal, *not* a purpose. Now, you can have a *purpose* for that money which should be to do something extraordinary that can benefit a lot of people.

Having that hot new car is a goal, *not* a purpose. Finding a man or women to have sex with is a goal, *not* a purpose. Wanting to learn the Game is a goal, *not* a purpose. However, empowering yourself through the Game to help empower others would be considered a purpose.

No one can give you your purpose. If someone gives you a purpose then you are living their dream and their ideal, **not** yours. You must define your own purpose and this is part of what makes the Game difficult, but powerful. In the Game you make yourself, no one else makes you.

Discovering your purpose can literally take days, weeks or months. But it should be a clear vision in your mind. You should be able to see it and it should also *move* you inside. It should be one of the first things on your mind when you wake up and one of the last things on your mind when you go to sleep.

A well defined purpose should be able to be summed up in one, and only one sentence. It needs to be that clear. If you cannot define your purpose in one sentence, then it is not clear enough. A purpose must be like the tip of a knife, small and sharp. This "knife" point will help you cut through all the other distractions that life will offer you.

Q: Now what about goals. Where do they come in?

A: Again, all goals should be aimed at accomplishing your ultimate purpose. If your goals are not in line with your purpose, you are spreading out your energy too thin and can be side tracked or even moved by a weaker force. This is a violation of the Game. You are not to ever be taken off of your purpose by anything outside of you, if humanly possible.

If I want to be a great father so that my children excel in life much further than I did and I decide this is what I'm going to live for, this becomes my purpose. Now I set my goals. I involve my children in anything that can give them an advantage over the average child to the best of my ability at all times. No excuse, no shortcuts, no distractions.

I may put my children through private school or even home school them. I may have them involved in the fine arts or sports. They become the center of my life, because they are my purpose. All the roads I travel, lead to them. I could go on and on in this example of how I could assist in my children's advancement, but I think you see my point.

Each step you take should get you closer to your purpose. If you are doing things that are not involved with your purpose, you are wasting valuable time and energy. And time is something you can never get back.

Now don't be ignorant about this and go shut out everyone and everything in your life. That's not living; life has its responsibilities, things that require our attention and time. But after those things have been taken care of, it's then time to get back on purpose. And this purpose is accomplished one goal at a time.

Once you decide on your purpose, then you form goals that will get you there. There is nothing wrong with changing goals. Sometimes new opportunities open up that were not there before when you originally made your plan. Sometimes you gain new insights and perspectives and this may change a few of your goals. Goals are not static and rigid, they are the weaker force and they are malleable. The problem comes when you change your purpose, your entire life then needs to be redefined.

Purpose is the ultimate form of commitment. It is something you should be prepared to die for.

Said another way, if you don't *stand* for something, you will *fall* for anything.

Q: Can you define commitment from the perspective of the Game?

A: Before I define that let me say this. If you are of weak character, your Game will be weak and easily crumble. You will look for excuses and justify not moving forward in your purpose.

You must learn to become unattached to outcomes, emotions and desires. When you attach yourself to these things, you can be controlled by them. If your entire life is based around becoming wealthy, then if someone offers you a large amount of wealth, you will break your principles and lower yourself to obtain it. You go from the dominant force to the submissive force. This has repercussions, Justice is always present. You should have no attachment to anything other than to your purpose.

Think about what you just read. Nothing in your life should be equal to your purpose, NOTHING. Not your mother, your father, your kids, your family, your wife or husband. Have some common sense here please, these people are of value to you but they are not equal to your life's final aim. This is why your purpose must be greater than yourself or you'll be easily distracted, led astray or fooled.

This is commitment. You must be willing to lose everything if it means fulfilling your purpose. That's a difficult pill to swallow, isn't it? This is why people run in and out of the Game and never accomplish much of anything. They are playing with the Game, instead of Playing (capital "P") the Game.

Going back to our drowning example, would you not risk your life to save your own life? If your life meant anything to you, of course you would. If you have no purpose, you are drowning in other people's desires, dreams and designs for your life. Save yourself. Commit to a purpose and let nothing or anyone steer you from it. And at the highest level of the Game, you must realize that the last sentence you just (*read*) also applies to yourself. Why? Because you can be your own worst enemy and your own greatest distraction.

CHAPTER FOUR
Principle Three: Reciprocation

The Principle – *You must give in order to receive. You cannot get something for nothing and truly call it yours. You must earn the right to have or possess anything in your life.*

Question: I must give in order to receive. What am I suppose to be giving? Can you explain this in more detail?

Answer: The answer to your question is best answered indirectly rather than directly. I will give you some examples. In order to receive the full benefit of farming you must till the soil, prepare the ground and plant seeds. Then you must nurture these seeds by ensuring that they will get enough water and sunlight. You are giving with the confidence that nature will do the rest and grow the crops.

If you want to receive the benefits of food you must prepare the food and eat. You must give yourself over to sleep to receive the benefits of it. You must give love in order to receive love. You must be the initiator, the starting point for whatever it is you want to obtain and nothing breeds nothing, that is Justice at work.

What you give must be given freely of your own free-will. It must be a decision you make because you *want* to make it. You can't eat if you don't open your mouth, put the food in and chew.

There are millions of people out in the world right now that want more out of life. Most of these people don't know what they want, but they know they desire more. But because they do not know what they want, they don't know what to give.

If you want more friends for example, you must put yourself out there and be willing to be a friend yourself *first*. This does not work the other way around. Some people will quote the Law of Attraction to you all day, but sitting and visualizing something is only one step. You must physically do something also.

Everything begins and ends with you. You know why? Look up (*from this book*) for a moment. Notice as you look around that everything in the entire universe at this point is literally revolving around you. You are at the center of your own world because everything is a certain distance from you.

Everything is about you. Not is an egotistical or selfish way, but in a way to make you understand that you must be the "cause" so that the desired "effect" will come.

What are you supposed to give? You give what you want to receive. To get love you give love. To get money, you must have something of value to sell and then give your time and energy selling it. To become better educated, you must give your time and energy to learning and study.

If you have no purpose then you have no goals. If you have no goals, then you don't know what to give to life. When you don't know what to give to life, you have no direction and can end up anywhere. Or worse, you can end up where someone else wants you to be.

Q: Can you give in the wrong way?

A: Yes you can. Anytime you interfere with another person's will-power, no matter how you're giving, you are in violation of the Game and will be held accountable for your Justice.

Q: What if another person is in the way of me accomplishing a goal or working toward my purpose?

A: Life has a rhythm to it. Unless that person it 100% concentrated on your downfall or destruction, just the fact of you remaining on your path will overwhelm whatever negative energy they throw at you. Remember, a weak force cannot stand up against a **consistent** strong force. This is called keeping your "Game Tight".

This is where your strength of Character comes in and is tested. Just because someone is in the way do you give up? NO! Do you move them out of your way by force? NO! You must stay on point and focused and Justice itself will move them out of the way. Their intentions toward you are negative and therefore when that energy cycles back to them, the downfall they wanted for you will come back to them instead. This is why you appreciate your haters; they are removing themselves out of your life with no effort from you. You don't even have to spend any energy on them at all. What you resist, persists (as they say). By them resisting you they are giving you their attention (energy) and time. When a person gives you their attention and time you remain a force in their life, something of significance, even if they hate you.

If you do give haters attention (energy) you are dividing or spreading your energy thin, and this weakens your force. In the Game we call this a "Game Leak". If you leak too much Game you are liable for "Game Loss" – losing what you've gained.

Never become a hater yourself. That energy is self defeating, literally. When you look at the accomplishments of others, don't look at them in envy or jealousy. Instead realize the truth. The truth is, if they have it, you can have it too. All you have to do is give what is necessary.

Q: You said I must give to earn the right to have something. And then you said I cannot interfere with another person's will-power, so are you saying I can't persuade someone to do something? Even if it's for me and can help me achieve a goal?

A: First and foremost, you can never earn the right to possess another human being. If they, completely of their own free-will, submit themselves to you then that is fine and is in perfect respect of the Game. The disclaimer here is – you must let them know **all** the risks involved upfront. You must be brutally honest and make sure they completely understand *everything* involved. You must give them the choice.

We submit our free-will to people all the time. If you decide to get on a public transportation bus, you are submitting your will over to the driver. You are trusting that he or she can drive safely. Same thing when you go to a restaurant, you're trusting the food you're eating is safe. You're life is literally in someone else's hands. We know the risks upfront although we don't consciously think about them.

Persuasion is the act of influencing someone to do something or change their beliefs, attitudes or behaviors. If you are up against a person of weak will (little will-power), you can probably convince them to do things they are not comfortable with. This will trigger Justice though, but it is up for you to decide if you want to deal with the consequences of your actions.

Never forget, everything has a price!

If you force someone to do something, either through physical force, the threat of violence or death, or through mental abuse this extracts a heavy burden and a high price.

Going back in history, the King never executed someone personally; he gave someone else the order. But just because he didn't physically perform the execution, he was still responsible for the Justice because *he* gave the order. Remember, it is not just what you sow, but what grows from what you sow. No one can escape Justice.

I would be lying if I said that there is no manipulation in the Game. There are certain degrees of manipulation in almost everything. What do you think a television or radio commercial is? They are trying to persuade and manipulate you into thinking about their product in hopes that you will purchase it. Do you really believe politicians are showing you who they really are? They are "Running Game" on the masses.

Before you persuade and manipulate you must ask yourself if you are ready to reap the consequences of that. That should be the first question you ask yourself.

Q: You're confusing me. You just said that manipulation is a part of the Game, but before you said the Game is brutal truth and honesty. Which one is it?

A: Both. I need to emphasize this again. The Game does not care how you use it. The Game is just there to be Played.

You have to ask yourself if you can stand the heat of the fire you are about to ignite. It's your choice, your will-power that makes that decision.

Manipulation may be part of the Game but so are brutal truths. You never have to manipulate and persuade if you choose not to. But you can be honest. You can both time your truths and carefully place your honesty. This is another lesson so I will not go into detail now. Next question.

Q: Can't giving to someone be considered a form of manipulation?

A: It can be, it depends on your **intention** behind it. If your intention is to manipulate, then yes – if you give to someone freely with no hidden intentions or expectations in return, then no.

Q: Let's get back to self-empowerment now. How do I know I have the right to something?

A: You have the right to any and everything in this world. The problem is that people will only except or expect what they believe they deserve. As long as you're willing to pay the price for what you want, you can have it. As long as you are willing to give everything that is necessary to get it, you earn the right to it and it's yours.

People will spend hours formulating a plan to buy a new cell phone. They will look up the costs of the phones they like, compare features, see how much money they need to save and then go through the process of purchasing it. But when it comes to bettering their life as a whole, they do nothing. Self-empowerment is the same process just on a larger scale.

If you can plan to acquire something as insignificant as a cell phone, you can plan and do what is necessary to make major gains in your life. You just have been conditioned not to and are afraid.

Great people did not start out great, they became great. They started with a purpose and gave what was necessary to achieve what they wanted to achieve. You can do the same thing. And through the understanding of the Game, the process is even easier because you will know what you're doing and where you are making your mistakes.

Change your mind and get yourself a purpose. Work toward that purpose and do what is necessary. It sounds so easy, because it really is. You just believe it's not, so to *you*, it's not.

You want the best, so give the best. Weak effort breeds weak results. You don't want to Play the Game just to get by, you want to Play to Win. Keep that in mind.

Remember this rule of the Game:

When you gain something you lose something else.

Sometimes this loss is only time or energy. Sometimes this loss may be money or resources. There is an old Sicilian saying that goes, "You lose the bait when you catch the fish," This is an easy way to remember this rule. This is the other side of the coin when dealing with reciprocation.

CHAPTER FIVE
Principle Four: Perception

The Principle – *Perception is King and emotion is Queen. How you look at things and events will determine what they mean to you. Perception can open and close doors.*

Question: What do you mean by perception is King and emotion is Queen?

Answer: Going back to the structure of the Game, we need to take that and internalize it. Meaning, we need to look at what's inside of us as a pyramid structure also.

Our mind controls our body. Our mind formulates thought and those thoughts shape what we do and say.

People act and speak the way they think.

If you want to truly know about a person, you listen to what they say and then look at what they do. People can put up a good front, but over time, or when put in a stressful situation, the real them will come out. It *has to* because of the way they think.

You have the conscious mind or the mind that functions when you are awake; the thinking and analyzing part of your mind. You have the sub-conscious mind, the part of your mind that operates below your awareness. It remembers smells, things you see and things you hear and stores anything your conscious mind cannot analyze at any given moment. You also have an emotional side of yourself.

Your conscious mind is King because it is through your conscious mind that you perceive things and analyze them. It is the judge. Two people can go through the same experience but perceive them completely different.

Example: You are looking at the news on television and see that someone robbed a bank. This is when your conscious mind kicks in. You may say that this person is a criminal, a thief and deserves to be dealt with by the law. But another person may see this same news broadcast and think that maybe that man or women was desperate. Perhaps they were not intelligent enough to find a better way to get money to feed their children. They did something wrong but maybe it was for a good reason. Two different perspectives, same event.

Your King should perceive and judge events with logic and reasoning. Now let's look at the emotional side of you, the Queen.

Example: Same news broadcast as our first example. Now if you perceive the bank robber as a criminal and thief, the emotional side of yourself may feel anger or a slight hatred. The other person who saw the broadcast and had a different perspective may not feel anger at all, they probably feel sympathy and pity for the bank robber. Two different emotional responses coming from two different perspectives.

The way you perceive things will control how you emotional respond to things – the majority of the time.

If you are told all your life that you cannot accomplish anything, that will become a perception of yourself. And whenever you are called to do something out of your comfort zone, you will be so overcome with doubt and fear in your abilities that you will likely not even try.

The King should control the Queen. You should not let emotions control your perception and reasoning (the Queen controlling the King).

Q: So basically you are saying that we should keep our emotions in check?

A: That's exactly what I'm saying.

Q: So do you mean we are supposed to be emotionless?

A: No. We are human and we have emotions, you just don't base your decisions off of emotion. You should never make a decision when you are emotional. It will 90% of the time be the wrong decision.

It is fine to feel emotions and recognize them, just don't let them change your perspective. The King should always rule properly from his throne. The Queen must respect the King's position at all times.

When you detach yourself from outcomes it is much easier to look at things with logic and reason and take the emotion out of it. If you are an emotional person, you can be easily misled, manipulated and used. This is a serious "Game Leak".

Q: So how should the King rule over the Queen?

A: According to the Game, the story of Adam and Eve in the Bible holds a symbolic significance. In the biblical story of Adam and Eve, Eve was the personification of the weaker or submissive force. She was the one who was easily manipulated by the serpent. She was easily misled because the serpent appealed to her emotions, her desire to be great and god-like; her vanity.

When you are led by your emotions, you are allowing your Queen (emotion) to rule over your King (perception). You make decisions with clouded judgment and haste. Decisions made out of emotion are usually destructive, to yourself and others. Just like when Adam listened to Eve and ate the fruit. The decision that caused that action is considered the fall of man.

In history every ruler was considered to be chosen by god or "the gods," depending on the culture. It was a King's divine right to rule. The King was the height of power, but he was not above god or "the gods" (depending on the culture).

To control the Queen your King must respect a power greater than himself, god. In the Game, god is your purpose.

Your King should base his judgments off of whether or not they are in line with the overall purpose and this will automatically keep the emotions in check because the emotions serve very little value when the mind is focused. Emotional responses to events are nine times out of 10 detrimental to the achievement of the purpose.

I'll say it again, basing decisions off of emotions is a Game Leak and if you continue down that road you will suffer Game Loss; losing what you've already gained.

In hip-hop culture it is considered very disrespectful to step on someone's shoes. And because this is the perception, when this happens, most people respond with anger. Even if the incident was an accident and the other person is innocent. This happens automatically because the King has been fed the perception of shoes being stepped on as disrespectful.

Q: So our perceptions can come from anywhere?

A: Yes and that is the problem. We let other people dictate how we should think. This thinking becomes our perspective and our perspective triggers our emotions.

Have you ever seen a movie that made you angry, sad or depressed? You may have even seen a movie that made you cry. Think about how powerful that is! Carefully crafted images and words on a screen so strong that it completely controls you. While you are watching that movie, you put god and King aside (your purpose and perception) and let someone else control it. You allow someone else to rule over your Queen. Just like how the serpent went directly to Eve first, he never spoke to Adam. He bypassed him completely.

Q: That's deep, I never thought about that. So what you're saying is you should always control your Queen by controlling your King?

A: Yes. To be in the Game, you have to change your perspective on things. That's what (*this book*) will do for you if you study (*this book*) and most importantly practice it.

(*This book*) will change your perception, not to make you a clone of me or anyone else, but to allow you to reprogram your King for greatness, so to speak, so that "you" arrive back to *you*.

Let me say it like this. When I told you that you will have to "die" to yourself and be reborn, this is what I meant. Your perceptions were given to you from school, media, parents, cartoons, movies, etc. To self-empower yourself you need to perceive things not how *they* want you to, but how they actually are. You need to accept reality and not fantasy.

The American dream is a fantasy – a good job that you work at until retirement. A house in the suburbs with a white picket fence and huge backyard. A two car garage and a television in every room along with two point five children. This is someone else's ideal of success. You accepted it as your dream because you didn't know any better. They "ran Game" on you.

If you want to get really deep, take the color yellow. Someone told you that color is yellow. How do you really know what that is? Science will tell you colors are nothing but reflections from the light spectrum. Your eyes take it in and your brain translates that frequency. You are told that particular frequency is yellow and that becomes your perception and therefore your truth. Your truth becomes your reality.

Q: So there are different truths?

A: Every person alive holds their own truth. But truth does not always equal reality.

According to a biography of European explorer (and businessman) Christopher Columbus, the Earth was believed to be flat during that time in history. This was mainly assumed by Catholic theologians. This concept of a flat Earth was accepted as truth, a truth that was not based on facts. But was this accepted truth a reality? Obviously not. Today we know it is an untrue fantasy.

You can believe with all your heart that there is no such thing as gravity – this would be your truth. But jump off a cliff and see what happens to you. Reality will meet you in less than a second on your way down. Now let's bring this closer to home.

Your average woman grew up watching princess movies and romantic comedies and this becomes their perception. They think this is how life should be. Men should act a certain way and be romantic like they are depicted in these movies and shows. Then when reality doesn't measure up to the fantasy, they are upset and disappointed. In their mind, these movies are truth and it becomes truth to *them*. But their truth, which is based on a lie, doesn't measure up to reality.

Q: So anyone who controls your perception can control you?

A: Yes. If you have no purpose and do not control how you perceive things, you can be led and will follow anything.

Q: Since women are considered more emotional than men, can (*they*) be more easily taken advantage of and controlled?

A: Yes. But this does not apply only to women. Any man who is over emotional can be easily controlled. Any Queen who is not kept in check by their King can be controlled by *anyone's* King.

It's like this. When you see a fast-food commercial on television and the burger is looking all extra good, juicy and tasty. If you give in to this image (fantasy) you will want one. You may not have even been thinking about a burger, but now you've seen it and now your mind attaches a thought to it. That thought is the perception of how good that burger is. You've had a burger before so you recall the taste. In only a few seconds you now want one. That thought became a perception. You perceive that burger as tasty and satisfying. That perception triggered an emotional response that means it gave you a desire. You now want that desire to be satisfied. Who just got Game ran on them? You!

To desire anything *is* an emotional response because desire *is* an emotion. Women are never satisfied (so they say) because they are more emotional and full of desires. But so are most men.

Now, this not a negative thing. This is part of a female's natural survival instinct which differs from that of a male, according to psychology. But that is another lesson.

A seasoned Player in the Game has a high degree of control over their perception and perspectives. This allows them to appear almost cold and emotionless. It is not that they are cold; they just don't allow their emotions to move them and alter their course.

Q: What is the reason for emotions then?

A: Emotions are to be used; you are not to let them use you. Again I'm not saying be emotionless, I'm saying use your emotions in a way that is a benefit, not a detriment.

Use your emotions to fuel your purpose. When you think of your purpose you should feel something. You should feel joy and hope, maybe a sense of freedom. You should feel love for those you care about and be generally happy about having another day on this planet. It is ok to feel, just don't become over emotional and base your decisions off of that.

I'll repeat it again, here's why. If you constantly base your decisions off of emotions then anyone with Game that knows that, can stir you up and lead you to where they want you to be. Great speakers all throughout history knew how to stir emotions. They have mastered the language to such an extent that they can bypass your King and influence your Queen. Is this right? It depends on the speaker's **intention**. But now that you know the Game, you should think twice about being emotionally moved by anyone if what they're saying doesn't apply to you. That sounds harsh, doesn't it? I told you the Game is brutal honesty.

There is *nothing* wrong with being educated and learning from people who are operating at the level you want to be at. You cannot empower yourself if you are ignorant. But if they are not teaching anything of value and you are not learning anything of value, then they are just running their mouths. At this point it is your duty to "peep" Game and protect your King and Queen.

CHAPTER SIX
Principle Five: Value

The Principle – *The idea of value is one of life's most powerful motivators. When you value something you will go through more trials to have it and accept more from it. If you do not value yourself, no one will value you.*

Question: How does value work in the Game?

Answer: Value is the cornerstone of the Game. It is the great motivator. It is the perception of value that creates desires and stirs the emotions. Through the perception of value you can tear apart other people's Game (peep Game) and see the truth (or reality) in it.

People will sacrifice things they *need* for things they *want* if they feel it has value. Hundreds of thousands of people flock for the release of new shoes, new clothes, the latest cell phones and even video games because these things hold value to them and their social circle.

What is value exactly? Value is a fantasy, an ideal. It is a perception of something, not always the reality.

This perception is true maybe only 25% - 50% of the time. There are things in this world of value that should be valued but even then, it depends on a person's perception. A 500 year old painting is valued, but only to those that accept that perception.

Value in the Game is not an external thing but an internal one. Value is something you make yourself into so that it can manifest outward. One of the keys to self-empowerment is being of value. You should have a use, people should benefit from knowing you and being around you. You should be adding and elevating their lives, not taking from them. This makes you valuable. Also, the more you educate yourself about things and the more experiences you have, the more valuable you become.

Look at it from this perspective. Let's go back to the example of us drowning. Our life is at stake and we call out for help. Now if someone jumps into the water and rescues you, that person's skill has tremendous value; priceless. You could probably never return that favor to that person. That individual's bravery and skill in swimming at that point is unmatched. They added to your life, or in this case saved your life, and took nothing from you. How could you **not** want to repay this person if you had a way to do it? What if she or he rescued your drowning child? How valuable would that have been to you?

Value is what keeps the Game spinning because people sacrifice and put up with a lot of situations and complications just to possess something of value. This is the root of dependency.

Q: What is dependency?

A: Dependency is anything, whether material or immaterial, that someone will sacrifice in order to obtain.

If a person sacrifices paying their rent or mortgage in order to buy that new cell phone, that cell phone holds more value to them then their own living situation. This is pitiful but incidents like this happen all the time.

Dependency is almost like an addiction, a person feels as though they can't live without something. Either they feel they need it to improve the quality of their life or regain something they "lost" to improve the quality of their life.

You must understand, at the most basic level, people have two motivations. (1) They desire something and (2) They fear something. Said another way, this is gain and loss; attraction and repulsion. People may not want to win, but they damn sure don't want to lose. They don't mind gaining as long as they don't have to try too hard. And they don't want to lose if they can help it.

People want things to be easy. People are inherently lazy. Gain and loss (desire and fear) are ever present when it comes to dependency.

When you mix perception (King) and emotion (Queen) you get a third quality – a child called dependency.

Here are the top 12 major dependency points in people's lives:

(1) Food
(2) Clothing
(3) Shelter
(4) Security/Safety
(5) Communication/Relationships
(6) Sex
(7) Entertainment
(8) Mental and Emotional Well-Being/Spirituality
(9) Wealth/Saving Money

(10) Living Better (health/medicine)
(11) Admiration/Power/Prestige
(12) Convenience

These are the foundation of what people will sacrifice in order to have. And these are what people fear to lose. These are the things people covet and put value into. There are more, but like I said, these are the top 12, the most important.

Now sit and think a moment about things you value and you will discover that they fit on this list somewhere. We don't want a new car just to want it. We may want safety (4) and the prestige of being seen in something brand new (11).

We want to go out and meet people because we want to improve our relationships or find someone to start a new one (5). And in the end, almost all new relationships with people who are attracted to each other end in sex (6).

People smoke cigarettes because they are addicted, and as twisted as it sounds, cigarettes fulfill their sense of mental and emotional well being (8) and it is a way to de-stress that is convenient (12).

When you are dependent on something to fulfill one or more of these 12 points, it becomes valuable to you. You will sacrifice to obtain it, because you desire it, because you perceive it as necessary for your life (King and Queen under a false god – a weak purpose and goals).

These 12 points work the opposite way as well. People do not want to *lose* these things. People do not want to lose their sense of safety and security (4), or lose a relationship (5).

Peep Game.

Every coin has two sides; you are to never ignore one side of the coin because you may miss something crucial.

Q: So in the Game we become valuable, how is that done?

A: I already answered that. You must add to people's lives in such a way that they *want* you there. You are not a burden but an inspiration. You don't just take, you also give. You exchange your time for their time, your energy for their energy and you allow access to your resources in return for access to theirs. They don't need you and aren't dependent on you (that's goes into the Game's "dark side") but they respect and appreciate you. This makes you valuable to them. Remember to never push this too far because you will be in violation of the Game, you will be interfering with their will-power.

When you have Game, you have solutions. You understand *why* people do things. You understand desire and dependency. If you truly examine yourself, you will see how other people think as well. This is not easy, people hate being introspective and holding the mirror up to themselves, but this is the price you must pay to becoming a major Player (Boss Player).

When you are able to help and assist other people you become valuable to them. Why? Because you have solutions to their problems. You will understand them in a way no one else can and you can help them overcome their weaknesses and provide them strength. This only comes when you do this for yourself *first*. Again, this is the price you must pay. This is the work you must put in. This is the death of "you" and the rebirth of *you*. Not everyone is able to accomplish this.

As you learn new things, educate yourself and take on new skills in pursuit of your purpose you will find that your greatest resource is not money, but people. When you are in the Game, you invest in people. Everything you can ever want to do or accomplish in life must be done through people at some point or another.

The more you master the Game, the more valuable you are and the more people will be willing to invest in you. Remember you must give in order to receive. By sincerely investing in people they in turn will invest in you. But in order for that to happen, you must become a person of value first and foremost.

You need to realize, there are things in people's lives that take. Working takes time and energy, mates and children take time and energy, family takes time and energy. People have to eat, deal with other people's negative moods and attitudes. People have to stretch their paychecks in order to do something that brings them only a few hours of joy. Everything in their life takes. When you are in the Game, you are something that gives.

Q: Still not getting this. What are we supposed to be giving? Game?

A: This depends on how you choose to Play the Game. You can give any of the twelve dependency points or help people not to lose them. You can educate them on how to obtain them as well on how not to lose them. Doing this takes up your time, energy and it can even take up resources.

Remember, you are in motion. You are moving for a cause greater than yourself, your purpose. You must give what is necessary to obtain your purpose and that includes what you give to people. This may seem unclear to you because you are not Playing the Game yet.

People naturally respond to problem solvers. People want solutions to their problems. When you have Game, you are a natural problem solver because you have solved your own problems. I'm not trying to confuse you; I'm trying to change your perspective on life. I am also not trying to give you a step-by-step formula (quick-fix) because then you won't be Playing the Game *your* way, you'll be playing it *my* way.

Peep Game. People who have been through hardships get worn down and get tired of being strong for everyone around them and themselves. It is a breath of fresh air when someone cares enough to help them. Not everyone will appreciate it, but those that do will help you "Expand your Game". They will help you achieve your goals.

What you are doing is breaking people's mundane daily routines and disempowering mental patterns which we'll discuss later (*in this book*).

Look at a millionaire, how do you think they achieved that status? If they made their money honestly, they added value to thousands of people's lives, maybe more.

Look at a rock star, pop star or rapper. They add value to people's lives and reap the rewards for doing so.

This is how the Game works. You cannot get something for nothing.

When you help people you start the cycle of Justice and when it comes back around it comes back in full force. Everything that grew from you giving to someone else will come back to you sooner or later. Remember, not just what you've done, but everything that grew out of what you've done. This works for the positive and negative. This is why it is so important to Respect the Game. When Justice comes back in full, you want to be there to receive. But you must be consistent and stay on purpose. When you alter your purpose you change course and all the work you put in will come back. But because you changed course (have a new purpose), what comes back will have little benefit to you. It is wasted energy and wasted time. I hope that makes things a little more clear.

I know I went on a slight tangent there, but there are so many ways to answer your question. To keep all of this as simple as possible just remember three things – **time**, **energy** and **resources**. There are many more ways to give but these three are very easy to remember.

Q: Time and energy, ok I get those, but what are resources?

A: A resource is a "supply" that can be used when you need it. Money can be a resource, giving help or aid can be looked at as a resource, giving support can also be a resource. Knowledge and information can be invaluable resources. And yes, even helping people solve problems is a resource – in fact, that ability is called being resourceful.

People you know are connected to other people, places and things. These people can provide things to you at discounts or even free. They can get you into places you normally couldn't get into yourself. And they know other people that can do the same thing. In the Game of business, people call this networking. But it really is just having access to things when you may need them – a supply.

When you allow other people access to your resources, you are connecting them to money, aid, support, knowledge and information or to the people in your "network". And you form your "network" by giving the time, energy and resources you currently have available. As your Game expands, so do your resources.

Q: I think I get it. So by empowering ourselves, we become valuable to others. We help them and this value will get others to help us? Right?

A: You have the right idea. It is an investment, like investing money. You expect a return at some point and when you invest in people it is the same concept. You are investing your time, energy and possibly resources. You definitely deserve these things in return.

Q: So something of value is something people feel they cannot be without or don't want to lose.

A: That's correct.

Q: So how do we investing in people? It sounds like a lot of work.

A: It can be, but again it depends on how you Play. You can affect thousands of people through one song. It doesn't have to be a personal one on one sit-down if that's what you're thinking.

You can write great music, write great books. Do stage-plays or screen plays that are more than just entertainment, they have a message. A deep message that hits home. A message that bypasses a person's King and speaks to their Queen. You want to move people emotionally. This is high level Game. Value is almost like the prince of the Kingdom. He has almost the same powers of the King, but he cannot sit on the throne. He does however, have power to influence the Queen. It is in his birthright.

Your value depends on the other person's perception; it is nothing that can be forced. They have to, of their own free-will, perceive you as someone of value. Not everyone will and that's fine. Don't focus on those that don't, focus on those that do.

The world works off of value because the world works off of the Game. If you are going to play then Play to win. Be of value, create valuable things and your world (social circle) will not be able to get enough of you.

CHAPTER SEVEN
Principle Six: Advancement

The Principle – *Anything that does not grow and changes, dies. In life you should be constantly progressing, learning and experiencing new things. Advancement is growth into bigger and better situations in life.*

Question: What is advancement or growth exactly?

Answer: Everything in nature is born, grows, declines and eventually dies. Growth is expanding your Game. If your Game is not expanding, it will die.

Every great empire and kingdom on earth went through the natural phases of birth, growth, decay and death. This is the nature cycle and rhythm of life. If you are not constantly on your purpose, all the time and energy you put in will die out. All the cycles you started will come back and because you did not keep starting new ones, the flow will stop.

Your Game does not stop until you accomplish your purpose. And your purpose should **not** change until you accomplish it. Once your purpose is accomplished, you have reached the height of that Game and can then begin a new one, with a new purpose. Some people will take their entire lives trying to achieve their purpose and that is perfectly acceptable. If or until that time comes, you must constantly be working toward your purpose everyday as much as humanly possible. You don't stop and you don't **fold**, you **function**.

Q: Fold?

A: The concept of Fold or Function is easiest to explain like this. If we are running in a race and you trip on the way to the finish line do you just lay there on the ground? No, you get up and continue to run. Laying there is foolish and accomplishes nothing. And yet people do this everyday. They are working on their goals, pursuing their purpose (if they have one) run into resistance and just stop. They Fold. In the Game you must always Function, never Fold. You must keep moving and allowing your Game to grow (expand), otherwise, what's the point of it all?

The concept of Fold or Function builds character. Life is a series of problems; your duty is to find a solution to each problem. To solve a problem, you must get to its root.

Q: How do I find the root of a problem?

A: Through our good friend negation. You must go through what something is *not* to get to what something *is*.

Q: Ok then, how do I negate?

A: By asking yourself questions. Every problem has a root cause. It could be one thing, it could be a few, but there is always a root.

Think of a car. Every piece of a car works with and affects something else. If one system in a car malfunctions it may still run, but eventually that system will affect another system. It works like the body. Each system in the body works with other systems, if one system begins to break down, it puts strain and stress on the other systems.

When we look at an onion, it has layers. You can keep pulling layers back until you get to the core of the onion. And that is negation. Peeling back layers, looking through the "systems" of a problem seeing what affects what and eventually identifying the root of the problem – what started the other systems to fail.

Q: When Playing the Game, we don't Fold we Function. Can you explain more what functioning means?

A: Simply it means that always looking for the easiest road to a goal (or your purpose) is a sign of cowardice. You must be willing to go through hell to get to heaven. You cannot always move in safety and fear because you will never fully commit. If you never fully commit you will likely never succeed.

To Function means to stay "Down and Dirty" in the Game, to never surrender or fall weak. We all make mistakes, mistakes are **not** falling weak. When you do not bounce back from your mistakes, **that** is falling weak. I don't know how I can make this any clearer.

Keep your Game Tight and stop looking for shortcuts and quick fixes. This isn't playing the Game, that's *limping* in the Game. We're trying to *run*.

As you're solving problems and examining failing systems you must always look for the best solution. Not the easiest. And please, if you're in the Game do not put the new onto the old and expect it to work like something new. That's like putting a new engine in an old car. Yes it's going to run for a good while but the old parts will begin to speed up the wear and tear on the new. Function! Give 100% all the time. Put your best foot forward all the time. Respect the Game.

If you are Functioning, your Game with grow and expand like it's supposed to. Justice is at work here.

Functioning is nothing but **persistence**. You don't stop for *any* reason. Despite the problems, the hardships, the rejections and the losses, you never Fold. You stay persistent and focused. You always wield your dominant (strong) force and let it conquer the weaker forces. It may not work when you want it too or when you feel it should, but if given enough time and room, it will overcome *everything* in your path in its own time and natural rhythm.

Another point I would like to stress here is that you should always take pride in everything you do. Even when you are doing something you don't enjoy, you still take your time to give it the attention and effort it deserves. Your Game is a reflection of you. You don't want it to be a brochure; you want it to speak volumes like a set of encyclopedias.

Q: How can I tell if my Game is growing or expanding?

A: Through the understanding of progress. If you don't know how to measure progress, you are once again limping in the Game.

Progress is reaching your goals one by one by one. If you have no purpose, then you have no goals. When you have no goals there is no way to measure progress.

Remember, you have an overall purpose and to achieve this purpose you have goals. Goals are like the alphabet – A, B, C, D all the way to Z. You cannot go straight from A to Z and skip the letters in between. That is not reality. Each letter (goal) is important and all the letters must be present or there is no complete alphabet (purpose). An incomplete alphabet has no use; you cannot have a complete language without all the letters. I hope that makes sense.

So when measuring progress you look at how each goal is being accomplished. Once a goal is complete you move on the next. You complete that goal and move on to the next until your purpose is achieved. And once your purpose is achieved (and **only** when it's achieved), you create a new one. Then this new purpose will have goals that must be completed and the cycle starts all over again. Some purposes are so great that they may take a lifetime to achieve and that is perfectly acceptable.

I'll give you a very simple example. Let's take a common housefly. The male housefly's entire purpose in life is to mate with at least one female before it dies. The lifespan of the male housefly is about 90 days but they seldom live longer than a month. Houseflies are prone to running into predators.

Now in order for the housefly to live long enough to mate it needs what? The male housefly needs food, air, room to fly around so that it can find a female, an optimal temperature and to avoid predators. These are all goals – Finding food, being able to continue breathing, being unconfined so that it can seek a female, not being where it is too hot or too cold (to keep its body from shutting down) and staying clear of anything that will kill it.

If the male housefly does not accomplish *any* of these goals he will not have achieved his purpose and his life will have no meaning. If the housefly fails to accomplish just *one* of these goals, he may still achieve his purpose (unless he is killed), but the odds will be stacked against him.

Your Game is only expanding and growing if you are continually hitting goals on the way to your purpose.

Q: I forgot to ask this earlier but you mentioned rhythm and natural rhythm a few times. What is rhythm?

A: Actually this is a great place to discuss rhythm because it has a lot to do with advancement (growth) and measuring progress.

Rhythm is cycles or think of it as something that reoccurs at regular intervals. Life is not linear, it moves in a rhythm. It swings back and forth, or like a wave it rises and falls.

As applied to advancement, rhythm is the movement of your life in one direction or the rising of a wave. Once that swing reaches it maximum point, it will begin to swing back the opposite direction, or once a wave reaches its highest point, its apex, it will begin to fall.

Every cycle you start (Justice) works in a rhythm, it will swing all the way out and then swing back to its starting point. This is why you must always keep starting cycles because once the swing or wave stops, that's it – its work is finished. A cycle naturally reoccurs (keeps swinging back and forth) but it will lose momentum over time and eventually stop.

Now, you can continue to apply force to the same cycle allowing the swing to go back out again, or the wave to rise. The more force you "push" with means the further out the swing will be and the faster it will swing, or the higher and larger the wave will be and how much momentum it will move with. This is what Functioning (persistence) is, applying force over and over again to the same cycle.

When people teach on the Law of Attraction, which has become extremely popular over the last few years, they never teach you about rhythm which is one reason why the results are inconsistent.

Now, rhythm and *natural rhythm* are different. Natural rhythm is nature itself at work. The changing of seasons is natural rhythm. The passing of time is natural rhythm.

Your moods move in a semi-natural rhythm. Some days you feel energetic and have a great mood. Some days you are low on energy and are in a bad mood.

The rhythm of the cycles you start can be controlled to a certain degree. Your moods and emotions can also be controlled to a certain degree. You cannot control natural rhythm such as the changing of seasons and time.

Everything works on a rhythm. The rise and fall of an empire or a corporation – the ups and downs of a romantic relationship. All of this is a form of rhythm in action.

Rhythm is an advanced principle of the Game and it works off of other principles we haven't discussed. For now, this is all you need to understand about rhythm for self-empowerment, advancement and growth.

Q: I think I get it. So when you Fold, that cycle you started eventually just stops?

A: Exactly. When you give up on something, you lose the opportunity to receive what you were in the process of earning. This ends up as wasted time and energy. It becomes a leak in your Game. When you constantly change your mind, you have a major leak in your Game. Leaking leads to Game Loss.

Q: So is this why staying focused is good?

A: Yes when you are focused, you can remain consistent. When you are consistent with your decisions, you remain on top of your Game and can spot Game Leaks. When you spot a Game Leak you "plug" it by recognizing what is causing the leak and getting back to your purpose and goals. This is called, getting your "Game Together".

CHAPTER EIGHT
Principle Seven: Responsibility

The Principle – *You can only be accountable for yourself, you are responsible for everything you know and every possession in your life. You must be self-reliant.*

Question: I know what responsibility is to me, but I know the Game has a different perspective so let's hear it. What is responsibility?

Answer: Actually in the Game the definition of responsibility is similar to what it is in the dictionary. Responsibility is being accountable for what you do and what you know.

When you do not use what you know, it is **useless** to you. It's like having a freezer in your house but you just throw all the packaged meat on the floor. You could have preserved it but instead it's going to spoil.

You must be accountable at all times. You must be accountable for everything you do, say and think. This all ties back into Justice. You cannot fight Justice so you must learn to work through it. You own up to yourself and everyone who is in your circle (part of your life); the people that willingly help you expand your Game.

This is integrity and character. Being responsible adds tremendous value to yourself because you become a person of your word. Your word is your bond and you do everything in your power to never break it. This is wisdom also; you should never promise what you can't deliver. You should never open your mouth to agree to do something you know you don't want to do, or can't do.

When you are exercising responsibility you have the power to bring heaven and hell. Not literally, but people around you know that when you say something, you mean it. So if you say something good is going to happen, they can expect it to happen. When you say something bad is going to happen, they will expect that too. If you are well "seasoned" in the Game you can predict outcomes so when you speak it, you know it is already in the process of happening and when it finally happens, people will look at you in amazement. This is yet another reason the Game is so powerful.

When you truly understand Justice you can make predictions in your life and other people's lives.

Q: You said be self-reliant also. What is that?

A: Self reliance is just what it sounds like. You look inside yourself for solutions to problems. You look inside yourself for help. This does not mean you don't go find help outside of yourself, but you look inside of yourself *first*. You try everything in your power *first*. If you fall short, then you look for assistance outside of yourself.

This transition is a hard one to make sometimes because we are so used to immediate gratification. I can go to the computer right now and find information on anything. But when it comes to dealing with life's stumbling blocks and issues, you won't find those answers online. Those answers have to come from within. You must learn to depend and rely on yourself. How else can you expect other people to depend and rely on you?

You must be the example. When you are Game Tight, you are the most confident and "together" person amongst hundreds of others. A speck of pepper in a pile of salt.

Game is not something you do; it must be something that is inside of you. When the Game is inside of you it radiates out to other people. I guarantee you that when you start practicing and using Game people will look at you different. They have no choice, you will *be* different, you'll respond to situations differently. You will become a person that doesn't seek advice from them (people without Game); you seem to always have the answers.

In the Game we say, "You have no questions, but all the answers." This is a very lonely feeling. But again, this is the price you pay for the Game. You will only be truly understood by people on your "level". The average person couldn't really help you if they tried. They can't help you because you know their perspectives on life are not based on reality but on dreams and fantasies. You don't buy dreams.

Through the Game you will become a self-contained unit. You run Game but can never let Game be run on you. That is being an irresponsible Player.

Q: Can you explain what running Game means? Like when you say, "Someone ran Game on you?"

A: We have already talked about how everyone has their own truth, but that does not necessarily mean that it is equal to reality. When someone is running Game on you, they are trying to give you a fantasy, their version of the truth and make you accept it. This is what manipulation really is.

If you accept someone's fantasy over reality then someone ran Game on you. If you let someone make you feel that you hold less value than them, they just ran Game on you. If you allow someone to get an emotional response out of you, they just ran Game on you. This is the "dark side" of the Game. Once you know the Game you can peep this out and put a quick stop to it.

Never allow anyone to disrespect you. You check them, not with anger (or any other emotion), but with Game. You logically and eloquently use your mouth-piece and check them. At this point Game will recognize Game and if both of you are Players, you can then speak the truth to one another. You can then move on with mutual respect. This is how the Game is supposed to be Played, but don't expect everyone to respect the Game.

I've said this before but I'll say it again. There is nothing wrong with being humble around those who have more Game (or more knowledge about a subject) than you so you can "soak it up". You should want to learn and grow as an individual, just don't humble yourself so much that you are led by them. Unless that is what you choose to do of your own-free will, **not** because Game was ran on you. Even the King had a group of advisors who saw things he couldn't and knew things he didn't know. He listened to them and considered their advice; this didn't make him any less a King because he always made the final decision.

Q: Sorry, that reminds me of another question I always had, what it the mouth-piece? I know it means the way you say things, but does it means something deeper?

A: The mind is the most important tool in the Game. Remember I taught you that people act and speak the way they think? Well this applies to a person with Game.

A Player has three main tools. Their mind, their body and their mouth-piece. The mind is their perspective, the use of the Game. Players dress well and look well because this is a reflection of what's inside of them, greatness and power. Looking well and dressing well also distinguishes you from the everyday average person. And lastly a Player speaks intelligently because they have Game. They use their mouth-piece to open and close doors (invite people in and keep people out).

SIDE NOTE: *If you want to sharpen your communication skills pick up my book, <u>Holding Magnetic Conversations</u>. It will explain in detail how to use your mouth-piece to talk to anyone, anytime, anywhere. It's simple and can be learned in hours.*

When you have Game you don't act and speak like everyone else because you don't think like everyone else. If you go up to the average person, smile and give a sincere, "Good morning!" I mean really mean it! Most people will look at you like you've lost your damn mind. And that's how the Game is, you are so sincere and honest with everything you do and that positivity (being sure of yourself) is so strong that people will think you lost your damn mind.

You don't feed negativity; you disperse it with stronger force. At your job you always have that *one* person that complains all the time. You don't sympathize with them, you raise them up to your level and if they cannot (or refuse) to come up to your level, you avoid them. They are a waste of time and energy. A useless cycle, a wasted investment. Now that sounds cold, doesn't it? Again, this is the price you pay.

I'm not saying be rude to them, I'm just saying don't feed them anymore time and energy than necessary.

No worries though, water seeks its own level.

Q: I've heard people say that before, "Water seeks its own level," What does that mean when it comes to the Game?

A: In science it basically states that if there is no outside force acting on water, it will always level out. I always use the example of pouring water into a bowl. Even though you pour water into a bowl on one side, the water will even out and become level on the surface when you stop pouring. This isn't the best example but stay with me.

People say that this can be applied to people as well. "Birds of a feather flock together". People generally seek out and befriend people like them. While there is truth to that, the Game sees this on a deeper level.

Just like water (which can be both a weak and strong force) always desires to level itself out, people want to be level with people around them. The weaker force will try to match the stronger force. The lower will try to rise to the higher. The reality is, the weaker force will usually be consumed or dissipated by the stronger force, if the stronger force is concentrated.

When you have Game and are able to bypass a person's King (logic and reasoning faculties), you can raise their emotions (or lower them). Emotion is energy. Energy cannot be destroyed only changed in form. You must learn how to transmute (change) energy. You can change a person's sadness into joy. Fear into courage. Anger into calm. But again, you cannot do this in others until you master this *in yourself first*. Everything begins and ends with you, remember? Yet another price you must pay for self-empowerment.

A weak force responds to a stronger force not a weaker force.

It's like when you compare yourself to other people. You very rarely compare yourself to people doing worse than you; you compare yourself to people doing better than you. Why? Because the lower responds to the higher. Water seeks its own level; its lowest point wants to be level (even) with its highest point. Peep Game on that.

When you are the "highest point" around, people will naturally respond to you. This is part of what makes up your "aura".

Q: Going back to when you said you can change people's emotions, isn't that interfering with their willpower?

A: Willpower is the ability to choose what is right for you and what is wrong for you. They are like two equally matched fighters. Who wins depends on your intention and choices.

Everyone has willpower, imposing your willpower to limit another's choices or opportunities is a violation of the Game. The end result will be animosity; they will grow to despise you. You must take the responsibility for that and accept the Justice of that if that's how you choose to Play.

The highest level of the Game is self-empowerment and the empowerment of others. You must always give another person the ability to choose, you should never take their choice away from them. If you are elevating a person emotionally this is not a malicious act if your **intentions** are sincere.

Q: What do you mean when you say limit choices and opportunities?

A: If I threw you in the desert and took away everything you own except the clothes on your back and the shoes on your feet, your mind will immediately go into survival mode.

You know that if you do not find water and food you will die.

The problem in this scenario is that you have nothing to help you. You have limited resources. Because you have limited resources you have very little opportunities to get out of this situation alive.

Limited resources lead to limited options. And limited options lead to limited opportunities.

The lack of options and opportunities forces a person to use their natural survival instincts. This can force a person to accept and do things they would not normally do under better conditions.

When you empower yourself you are expanding your Game. An expanded Game means you have more resources available to you. In this example, I'll just talk about people. People are connected to their own resources whether it is knowledge, money, access to things and places. People also know other people with their own resources. This is why a person with Game invests in people first. It opens up doors because you have access to more resources and therefore more options and this leads to more opportunities.

I know you've heard the saying, "It's not what you know, it's who you know," from the perspective of the Game you must have something of value to get people to come to you first. And that something of value you give is **you**. The Game inside of you manifested outward. You help connect people to more resources and opportunities and they do the same for you. All roads lead to you and from you but you must understand, this comes at a price and requires you to take full charge of your responsibility to these individuals. It's not easy. Playing the Game correctly and respecting it is hard work.

Peep Game. The Game is not convenient, it can almost feel like a heavy burden and this is why I can give you all my Game and it will do nothing for you. People expect something for nothing and the Game does not operate that way. People don't want to carry the responsibility that self-empowerment bears. But to be a Player, this is required. You must be constantly Playing.

Q: So, to become a Player, where do I start? I mean this is a lot of information is there one principle I should start with or like something you can say to kind of bring all of this together?

A: Most definitely. Peep Game. If you do not know where you're going, don't take the next step. Also, a journey of one-thousand miles begins with the first step. Both of these measure the reality of wanting to gain something, and the fear of losing something. You take the next step when you are 100% sure where you want to go. When you take that step you must realize that the journey will be long and must be done step-by-step. There are no shortcuts in the Game.

So make your decision. Either you are going to step in the Game or step away from the Game. You have to do what is best for you. Either way, don't forget that you are responsible for what you know. You are responsible for the knowledge you have. Also never forget that when you have earned the right to something, whether knowledge or a material item, and you choose to not use it you *will* lose it. You must be responsible and **maintain** the things that are in your life. Everything needs time and attention (energy). This is Justice in motion and nothing escapes Justice.

These were the seven principles of the Game as they apply to self-empowerment. Now that you have a basic understanding about how the Game works we can move on to more advanced knowledge and concepts.

CHAPTER NINE
Examination of the Mind

Let's start with a reality of the Game.

Before you become, do or have anything in life, you have to know who you are first.

This is the **"Greatest wisdom of the Game,"** which leads to the greatest secret of the Game. Over our discussion of these advanced Concepts and Lessons you will begin to understand why.

Before we get into the Lessons there is something I must share with you. It is the "glue" that will bring all the Lessons together because you will be able to see how they all play and interact with one another.

The following Lessons themselves are only "surface" knowledge. I wrote them this way so that the average person could not take them and use them unethically.

What I'm about to share with you, if you truly understand it, will allow you to dig into the Lessons and Principles with tremendous depth. What I'm about to give you is the key to unlock the doors of Inner Game; the Game inside of yourself that you must manifest outward.

Even with this key, the average person will still not fully understand the Game until they use it to bring this entire book together. This is not something I can do for you. You must put in the work yourself to truly call yourself a Player.

Justice and Reciprocation are in motion here. Don't forget, you must earn the right to everything in your life to truly call it yours. That includes the Game itself.

You can't play a sport if you don't understand how to score, and what the rules are. You must learn these things and practice them. You can then go on to strategies on winning because you understand the basics. And if you have some natural skill, you may even excel in a few areas. This is the same way in the Game.

The Seven Principles are the foundation the Game is built on. The Principles may have sounded good and got you looking at things differently but now it's time to dig inside of yourself. Enough talk, the time to give you the key has come.

One of the Games Greatest Tools

When I speak to people about the Game, sooner or later they ask the magic question. It is usually something similar to this, "If the way I perceive something gives it a meaning to *me*, then how do I know I'm not selling myself a fantasy?"

What they're really asking is, "What makes up reality?" How do they know that when they change their perspective on something that they aren't fooling themselves? It's easy to say that gravity, heat, cold, dry, wet, hard, soft, etc. are realities. We experience these things on a daily basis. They are natural phenomena. But when it comes to the mind, how do we know the things we accept aren't just something we made up? Just because we believe something (or believe *in* something), does that make it just a truth or a reality?

Just by being able to think along these lines let's you know how powerful the mind is. If I lost you over the last few paragraphs, don't worry, over time it will make perfect sense to you.

The key I was talking about earlier is what will elevate your Game because you will begin to understand one of the greatest mysteries of yourself – The Mind.

The conscious (aware) mind works in patterns. Let me repeat that:

The conscious mind works in patterns.

If you were standing in front of me and I held up an object that was white, rectangle with four corners, was very thin, could easily be folded, had faint blue horizontal lines running across it and three holes down one side – what would you say it was? A sheet of notebook paper, of course. Now if I held this sheet up, how long would it take for your mind to decipher that this was a piece of paper? Less than a tenth of a second. There is almost no logic or reasoning involved. Your mind recognizes the **pattern** and returns a **conclusion**.

If you were driving along a street in America and saw a red colored octagon (eight-sides) with four white letters in the center with a white border around the edges, attached to a metal pole in the ground what would you say this was? A stop sign, correct?

Again, how long would it take for your mind to reach the **conclusion** that you saw a stop sign? Almost instantly.

Your conscious mind is constantly taking in everything around you. Everything you see, smell, hear, taste and touch.

Everything. The mind must defend itself by creating shortcuts. It needs to simplify the abundance of information into certain patterns so that it won't waste unnecessary time and energy figuring out **familiar** things. What is left goes directly into the sub-conscious mind – including **unfamiliar** information the conscious mind can't make meaningful sense of.

It's like when you're in the comfort of your own home; you know where everything is (for the most part). You usually set your wallet or purse down in a few familiar areas; same with your keys. Your clothes have their areas and so do your shoes. Now when you go to a new hotel for the first time, this pattern is broken. You don't know where to put your keys, your wallet or purse. You don't know where your shoes should go or your clothes. You're in the bathroom looking around for the soap, shampoo and towels. If you were at home these trivial things would take no thought because your mind established a pattern as to where these items were located. When you're in a new situation, this pattern is broken.

Do you see where I'm going with this?

Your mind works in patterns. People in the Game know this. Why do you think organizations around the world usually represent themselves with logos or symbols? This is how the mind works. Logos and symbols are patterns. Your mind will associate it with something and that association is usually what the creator wants it to be.

If you're training someone in a job they've never done before, the majority of that training time is spent with them establishing a new pattern. They are taking everything they're learning from you and putting it into a way that works for them.

Just like when a child is learning to walk. They fall, get up and try again, they take a step and fall and get up and try again. And this happens over and over until they get it right. Next thing you know, they're running. This child took it upon themselves to create a new pattern; this pattern was based off of what he or she saw around them – people walking.

The ability to walk upright is already in our DNA, but it doesn't register as "normal behavior" until it is seen. If a child grew up around a group of apes for instance, it would learn to move like an ape would. The ability to move our bodies in that manner is also in our DNA but it's not considered "normal behavior".

When you understand that the majority of your patterns are based off of what's around you, then you can begin to see why you think the way you do. If you grew up around wealth, wealth would be nothing special. It would be normal. This would be a reality to you. On the other hand, if you grew up in poverty and everyone around you was in poverty, this would be normal to you and you would accept it as part of your reality.

This is why you must always look at both sides of the coin. If you are in poverty, there is something keeping you there. And this is because of your mind's patterns. Your mind returns poverty thinking when you perceive things because this is a shortcut for it. But if you are in poverty and you see wealthy people, you now know there is another way to live. Your awareness has expanded which is good, but your patterns haven't changed and because of that, going from impoverished to wealthy will not happen (people act and speak the way they think). It can't happen until you change your **perspective** and create a new pattern. In this case it would be "wealth thinking" just to keep it simple.

People often use the term, "limiting beliefs". This is fine, but these beliefs come from a pattern in the mind. Remember:

A pattern is a shortcut that returns a conclusion about something familiar (normal) in your life.

People do not like to undertake new things because of the work involved in creating new patterns. I'll say this again, human beings may not try to win but they don't want to lose. Creating new patterns (the right kind of patterns) is winning.

People scream in joy at a baby learning to walk after a hundred or more failures, but they will not be willing to face a hundred failures trying to win at anything new (outside of their comfort zone). They developed the pattern that returns the **conclusion** that failure is bad. Let me help you form a new and better pattern now.

Life is the best teacher because you can learn from your failures and mistakes.

Failing is necessary to success! You will **not** succeed without failing. This is rhythm. As you get better and better through failing, the cycles of Justice you start will be sharper and more precise. As your cycles get better, the results will come quicker and be more accurate.

At first your patterns are incomplete so what you get back is a little piece here and a little bit there. But as you keep going and make the pattern complete, what you get back will be bigger, better and manifest faster.

Show me one man or woman who is a success in their life and ask them how many times they failed. And if they say they have never failed I will call them a liar straight to their face.

The mind works in patterns. What do you think habits are? They are patterns that play themselves out. If you have a bad diet it is because you have the pattern of eating unhealthy food. You eat unhealthy food without even thinking about it. Your mind plays the pattern out. Just like putting on a pair of pants, how hard do you need to think about that? Very little logic or reason is involved.

Half the battle is deciding to change your perspective. The other half is forming a new pattern to over-rule (overwrite) the old one.

Patterns are your King just doing his duties of managing the Kingdom with as much efficiency as possible. But, just because the King sits on the throne doesn't automatically make him the *true* ruler of his domain. Changing patterns, changes the way the King rules his kingdom. Changing patterns is the greatest tool of the Game which leads to the greatest wisdom of the Game, which eventually leads to the greatest secret of the Game.

In the next chapter we will delve into the system that keeps us powerless – how it works, why it works and how to "move and shake" (maneuver) through it.

CHAPTER TEN
Conditioning – The Concept of Direct and Indirect

Let's return now to the questions and answers session with our student from the earlier chapters.

Question: Where do our thoughts of powerlessness come from?

Answer: It starts from the time we are able to understand and comprehend the language. At that point, we have entered into the Game. Not our own Game, but the Game that the "outside" world plays.

You see, in order for a person or group of people to hold power they must have people beneath them. These people on the bottom must support the structure above them and they must accept being "ruled" over. This must take place consciously and sub-consciously. These powerful Players on the top largely condition you by running Game on your sub-conscious mind. They have us in a state of powerlessness by the time we hit our teenage years. We still behave like a child. And there are even grown people who still behave like children.

Children are dependent on other people's approval, instruction and acceptance. They desire to please others. Children also get into petty debates, arguments and disagreements. A child is used to asking others for help and for basic necessities. They are children and there is nothing wrong with this, they are unable to fully support and care for themselves. The problem is, due to conditioning, many of us never grow out of this child-like mentality. We want things our way – when we want them and how we want them. We desire to be protected and feel safe although the reality is the world is not that way. We are led by fantasies and ignore reality. To sum it up, we become **irresponsible**.

Q: So we are given fantasies to keep us dependant like children? That's what you're saying, right?

A: Not exactly. It's much deeper than just being sold fantasies. "Their" Game is much larger and deceptive than that. The best term I know is socialization, or social conditioning.

Socialization gives you weak goals, values and strips you of responsibility. Let me give you an example of how ridiculous this can get.

Let's take a young woman, say 25 years of age. Now it is "socially acceptable" for her to go to a beach in a bikini, walk around, get in the water, lie out in the sun and play volleyball. All this is considered normal.

Now let's take this same young woman and put her at home. The doorbell rings and she has to go to the front door. She may be wearing only a bra and panties, but she will cover herself up with a robe or throw on some clothes before she goes to the door. Now, it's "socially acceptable" to be half-naked on a beach in front of hundreds of strangers, but at home it's considered "socially *unacceptable*" to be half-naked in front of one or two strangers and even family. Why? Doesn't a bikini cover about the same amount of skin as a bra and panties? Why the change in behavior?

Well you say, she's at home, there is more risk of something terrible happening to her and she *should* cover up. I would say, fair enough, but you're missing the point. The point is it's ingrained in her mind that being half-naked at your front door is wrong, but being half-naked in a **designated** public place is better. She has been socially conditioned to respond this way and she does it because of the pattern laid out in her mind. And this pattern was likely taught to her by the same parents that let her wear bikinis at the beach when she was a young girl.

Another example. Let's take a young man around the same age of 25 and put him in a position where he must approach a young lady he finds attractive. Now his initial instinct is that he finds this young lady *physically* attractive, first and foremost. What else does he have to go on? He has yet to speak with her and determine her personality.

Now, if this young man is courageous enough to approach this young lady he will say everything *but* how he really feels and why he really approached her. He can't because it's not "socially acceptable". He can't just go up to her and say, "I came over here because of how great your breasts look in your low-cut top. For me, that is a serious turn-on. My name's Michael, what's yours?"

This young man is forced to lie, come up with excuses and be somewhat manipulative in his approach otherwise he'll look like a pervert. And he will do this without even thinking about it because he has the pattern in his mind that this is how things are. We are taught through social conditioning (socialization) to be indirect, **not** direct. Being indirect is a weak (submissive) force and being direct is a strong (dominant) force. The world in general is taught to be indirect.

Q: So indirect is weak and direct is strong. Can you go deeper into that?

A: Many of our mind's patterns come through us in an indirect way. Our parents teach them to us through their actions. Many of our parents tell us one thing but do things the direct opposite. Like telling us that we shouldn't use profanity, but when they get upset enough they are caught slipping out a few words. They try not to expose us to things that are harmful and pass on their values, but often times they don't live the life they advocate. That is the contradictory life of a Square. They pass on social conditioning and don't even realize why. And worst of all they don't question where it came from.

The majority of our social conditioning comes from school and the media. Many of us never had the opportunity to see a successful adult love relationship. So where do we pick up our ideals about relationships? From movies, novels and television.

I can take a man from America, born in the year 1910, and another American man born in the year 2000 and ask them, "Should a real man cry in public?" and they would both say no, 95% of the time. Now how do we have a gap of almost 100 years, and have two different men say the same thing? They learned that from somewhere. The man born in 1910 probably heard it from his father or male role-model growing up. If not, he heard if from his friends when he was younger. And the man born in 2000 probably picked this conditioning up the same way. I'm *not* saying men should cry wherever they feel like it. I'm just making a point about social conditioning. Are you following me?

We are conditioned indirectly and are taught to handle situations indirectly instead of directly. This is *one* of the biggest reasons that most people will never be empowered in life. They will set goals and never achieve them. They look for the easy route, the indirect route, instead of handling situations head on (directly).

Q: So we were conditioned indirectly and because of this we learned to do things indirectly?

A: Exactly. It's just like the young man who must use excuses and lies to approach a woman he finds attractive. He was initially motivated by her breasts, but he can't say that. It's like when you want to say something to a friend to help them. Some of the time you don't want to hurt their feelings or upset them. So you give hints and clues and "beat around the bush" until you see your opportunity to say what you really want to say. This can go on for days or weeks. It's ridiculous. This indirect approach strips you of responsibility.

When you are not direct, you don't have to be 100% responsible for your actions. When you are not 100% set on an outcome, when nothing extraordinary happens, then you can just come up with an excuse and not face the reality of a mistake or failure.

Once you give up personal responsibility you lose value. Not only that, you also lose the possibility of reciprocation and you set a weak cycle of Justice in motion. Indirectness is weak and so are the results. Please use some common sense here. Being and doing things *directly* is not always the best route to take. This takes wisdom, knowing when and how to apply directness. This is grace and finesse with the Game and it comes with practice. But whenever you're in doubt, it's best to go the direct route and be prepared to accept the responsibility for your actions. This makes you a King (or Queen) amongst men and women, and powerful amongst the powerless.

People who do nothing but work indirectly, no matter how successful they become, will eventually break under the pressure. Indirectness shows a person of weak character and when they are finally "tested" by people of strong character and integrity they will break. A concentrated strong force overcomes a weak force.

Q: So the "dark side" of the Game is being indirect with it?

A: No. There is plenty of directness even with the so-called "dark side" of the Game. It is just used to tear people down by poking at their weaknesses. It's like a bully in the school yard. Bullies are very direct. They will emotionally, psychologically and sometimes physically torture another child. These are all very direct, but look at the results. The bullied child loses self-respect and self-esteem and sometimes even more. This is a bully's goal and he does it directly.

A true Player operates directly as well. Instead of tearing people apart by their weaknesses, they help people strengthen their weaknesses. Both the "light side" and "dark side" of the Game use both direct and indirect methods to achieve their aims. The thing with social conditioning however is that you are indirectly taught to be indirect. So when the time comes to stand up for yourself, you don't really know how. This usually leads to lashing out emotionally or irrationally and you look either crazy or like a fool. Your outburst resembles that of a child. Or you run weak Game and try to act like a "victim" – another childish reaction. Socialization strips you of a lot of personal responsibility, and an irresponsible adult is almost like a child.

Q: You said earlier being indirect is like taking the easy route. What do you mean?

A: In the Game we say, "The distance between two points is a straight line. But that doesn't make it the best way to go."

Peep Game, pay attention I don't want to lose you. This is next-level (advanced) Game. Using the example of the straight line, the easiest route is the most direct route, are you with me? Obvious route, easy plan. But if there is **any** major obstacle in the way then continuing on that straight line would suddenly become inconvenient. Instantly you are faced with more options. When running up against this major obstacle, you now can:

(1) Stop and do nothing
(2) Turn around and go back
(3) Turn and go another direction all together or
(4) You can find a way **around** the obstacle and continue on your way.

What looked like the shortest and easiest route turned out to be more complicated than you had hoped. You started off with a single goal in mind and suddenly you have four choices in front of you. What do you do? That depends on your character and your force. I know all that probably sounded a little confusing so I'll simplify it.

Let's say you're putting together an expensive bookshelf. You have to put this bookshelf together piece-by-piece and all the pieces need to be screwed together. So here you are, putting this elegant bookshelf together and it takes you eight hours of hard work and attention to detail. After you're finished and you're ready to load it up with your book collection, you realize there is a single screw left on the floor. You missed putting that *one* screw in somewhere. Now what do you do? Do you take everything apart and look for your mistake? Or do you just shrug it off and hope the bookshelf doesn't fall apart at some point? So, what do you do?

Your mind, due largely to social conditioning, would get agitated at the prospect of taking apart and putting back together something that just took eight hours to complete. Your mind would formulate excuses and justifications all in an attempt to find the easiest route. Now here's the funny part. If you ignore that *one* screw and start putting books on the shelf and the shelf falls apart, you will go from frustrated to completely enraged.

Your mind has been conditioned to always look for the **easiest** route; the indirect one. Ignoring a serious setback (or problem) shows weak (submissive) character. You started off direct (strong) and then ran into a problem and then went indirect (weak).

The easiest route is not always the best route to take.

Just because you have to go around an obstacle or (in the example above) deal with a setback, doesn't mean you are not being direct. You are still on your goal or purpose; you just have to take another route to get there. You may lose some time, energy and effort, but the end results will be much better. If you're serious about being in the Game, life will throw tests like this your way *very* often. If you're always Playing, then you will always pass these tests.

Staying focused on your purpose and goals is direct. Changing meaningful goals because you are frustrated, fearful, doubtful or full of worry is indirect. You purposely changed your course just because you faced resistance. Let me tell you about resistance. Almost everything in life has resistance. Due to social conditioning you have been led to believe that things should happen fast. We can send information across the world in a matter of seconds. We can see pictures we take instantly. Technology is wonderful but nature does not work that way.

Trees do not grow over night. Certain flowers only bloom in certain seasons. Certain fruits and vegetables grow best in certain climates. It takes a child nine months to grow inside a woman's womb before birth. All of this is slow, and all of these *natural* occurrences face resistance. If you think that you will not face resistance in the world then you need to examine that part of your social conditioning. Children want instant gratification – a wise adult understands that everything has its own time and season.

Q: So is social conditioning a plan? Something made to keep us powerless or weak?

A: Social conditioning comes from a natural human survival mechanism. It is very natural to want to do what those around you do. This is part of human nature. At the same time, anyone who understands conditioning can use this to their advantage and have you behave and act in a way that renders you powerless.

Q: So that's like the "dark side" of the Game? Being able to manipulate people through human nature?

A: To a certain extent, yes. But again, both "sides" of the Game use direct and indirect methods, and some even at the same time.

In America, every four years we have a Presidential election. If the current President has served two full terms (eight years) then we have to elect a new President from usually two or three main choices. One from the Republican Party and the other from the Democratic Party and occasionally there may be one from the Independent Party.

So we are given a choice on who we want as President out of two or three options. But we are *not* given a choice as to who makes up these two or three options. We didn't get a choice, in the *choice*. Does that make sense? We are *indirectly* given a choice of the final candidates but we had very little say in who they were. But we are *directly* given the final choice – who we choose to elect as President. See the Game? We get the final option of two or three things, but we didn't get a say in the most important option – what two or three things we wanted to choose from to begin with.

Let me make this even simpler. You go to a clothing store and you're looking through the clothes. You are forced to make a decision from what is in that store. You don't manufacture the clothes and you don't own the store so you are forced to make a final choice from what's in front of you. Sounds almost trivial, doesn't it?

Here's how this works though. You don't control the fashions. So you may not honestly truly like **anything**. But you're forced to make a choice. That's like me coming to you and saying, "Hey! What are we eating tonight? Italian food or seafood?" Did you catch that? I gave you a choice, but you didn't have any part in the **original** choice of Italian cuisine or seafood. I *indirectly* gave you a *direct* choice. Either way I win. Whether you choose Italian or seafood I get what I want although *you* make the final "decision".

This sounds funny but what just happened is I ran Game on you. I won before we even started playing. I took away a part of your responsibility, altered your perception and you didn't even realize it.

Q: So directly being given choices is really an… illusion or fantasy?

A: It depends on who's "running" Game. Sometimes we need to be directly moved into things that benefit us. We may not see it's beneficial at the time. It's like convincing your child to do something they may not like at the moment but it's best for them in the long-run. Just like telling a toddler to stay away from a hot stove.

But when we take this back to our social conditioning you will see that of all the choices we think we have, we really only have a few and when we make them, we usually end up powerless.

I know this is a lot to "soak up" so I'll give you another simple example. It is generally accepted, through social conditioning, that you should follow all the laws of every level of government. But there are laws still on the books that you have no idea exist. Now let me make this clear, I do not advocate breaking the law! There must be a perceived structure in place or there will be chaos and unrest.

What I'm saying is that there can be hundreds of laws passed every year but we have no choice in what they are. We hand over that responsibility to elected officials.

When you turn on the television there are hundreds of channels to choose from, and once again, you must make a choice of what you want to watch. But you did not have a choice as to what programs run and at what time. You just make a choice from what is available.

On a certain level, this is settling. This is powerlessness. We move around in a world where many of our choices have already been made for us. Similar to how children are treated, don't you agree?

Q: So do we fight this or what can we do about this?

A: A Player is only concerned about how *they* play the Game. You cannot control everything. With that said, don't choose to be ignorant about things either. You should want to be aware of matters that affect you.

The reality is, those in power run things and the Squares uphold and perpetuate the structure. You must learn the Game, master it, empower yourself and then empower others. Then that empowered team or group can advance together.

Until there is a mass of Players who decide to change the current social conditioning, things will remain the same. The Players must become a dominant force. Until that time they will always be subjected to what the Square thinks is "right" and "good". But you can't blame the Square, they are in a state of powerlessness and they hate any change that is not "socially acceptable". It shatters their perception of reality. When your perceptions change, you must be responsible and make changes to yourself as well. Most people will never do that because that means they have to "grow up" so to speak.

Q: Many of their mental patterns have to be changed?

A: Exactly. You understand.

There is more you need to know so we will cover a few crucial Lessons before we close this book. You will learn about building self-confidence, becoming an individual of unshakable integrity and how to secure personal power and influence.

When something already exists, you cannot "build" anything new in its place until you get rid of what's already there – just like you can't build a brand new house in the same place where a house already sits.

In the following Lessons, you will break yourself down and then begin to rebuild yourself into a stronger, more powerful person. Let's keep it moving.

Now let's get into "you", so we can get *you* back to *you*.

CHAPTER ELEVEN
The Lessons – Getting "You" Back to *You*

LESSON 1: Standards & Core Personal Values
(Examining Yourself)

Defining your purpose through **core** personal values is not an overnight process. This is one reason why 95% of people will never define it for themselves. Either they don't know or they won't put in the work necessary for the results. Not putting in the work shows weak character. Why would you *not* want to do something to make yourself better? The only thing holding a person back are the mental patterns of complacency, fear, doubt, worry and lack of confidence.

We've covered the Principle of Value in this book as it applies to creating value of yourself so others can perceive you as valuable. But now we must discuss what your *personal* values in your life are. What's most important to you?

Later Lessons will help you form new mental patterns through changes in your perspectives. First though, you must examine where you are **now**.

You will take this journey inside yourself in three phases:
(1) You will uncover your Likes and Dislikes.
(2) Once you know your Likes and Dislikes you will discover *why* you like and dislike certain things through "general *personal* values".
(3) You will then dig further into your "general *personal* values" to discover your Standards. Standards are sometimes referred to as **core** (essential) personal values.

Phase One: Likes & Dislikes

Here's the exercise. This exercise works best when you are not tired, sleepy or hungry. You should have no food, alcohol or other intoxicants at least two hours prior to doing this exercise. Your mind must be free to roam and be as sharp as possible. Now, here are the steps:

(1) Find someplace quite and free of distractions. You do not want to be disturbed for at least an hour. Turn off your cell phone. No radio, no television. Send the kids to their Grandmothers.

(2) Grab a pen (not a pencil, you are not allowed to erase anything) and a piece of paper, on one side of the paper write "Likes" at the top. On the back side of the paper write "Dislikes" at the top.

(3) Take a few deep breaths, settle your mind and just write. Do not judge anything that comes out, don't second guess it, censor it or try to make it sound pretty. Just write. Write down your likes on the "Likes" side of your paper and your dislikes on the "Dislikes" side of the paper.

(4) This must be repeated. It is extremely important that you do not judge what you write! Do not censor it, change it or try to make it sound pretty. Just write. Just let whatever comes out just come out. Do not read what you wrote until *after* the hour is over. If you find yourself running out of room then grab another sheet of paper.

You never need to show this list to anyone. This is by you and for you only.

After the first few minutes you may find yourself straining to find more things to write, this is normal. What we are doing is gently refocusing the mind. Just keep thinking, "What do I really and honestly like, and what do I really and honestly dislike?" and things will begin to pop up. When they do, write them down immediately.

So, what's the purpose of this exercise? To learn yourself – to look at yourself as you've never looked at yourself before. After your hour is up and you go back and read over what you've written, if you did this exercise sincerely, you will discover things about yourself that you didn't know before.

This exercise brings out the deepest parts of you because when you write like this, it is the deepest part of you expressing itself – the part of you that is beyond emotion, logic and reason.

If you did the Likes and Dislikes exercise you should now have a general idea of the things you value, because you *Like* them. These Likes bring you joy, pleasure, peace or motivation.

Phase Two: General Personal Values – Understanding Your Likes & Dislikes

If you performed the first phase sincerely, you can now begin to pick out your "general *personal* values". These are things you enjoy spending time doing and things you wouldn't mind possessing.

It's once again time to get an hour of peace and quiet. Grab your Likes list and a few sheets of blank paper. During this hour you want to go over each of your Likes, one by one and ask yourself a very simple question.

"What benefit do I get from this?"

You should keep asking yourself this question about a single Like until you cannot formulate anymore answers. Write these answers down as they come to you. Again, do not over think, analyze or judge your answers, just write them down. Once you've exhausted your answers move on to the next Like and repeat the process. Refocus the mind and hold it to the work in front of you.

This process is extremely important because it will help not only define yourself but it will lead you to discover your Standards. Don't stress yourself over this; just take it one hour at a time. I would not recommend doing more than three hours in a 24 hour period. Depending on the length of your Likes list, this process can take days or weeks and that is perfectly acceptable.

What you will come to realize is that your Likes alone are *not* that important. Your Likes are only as important as what they give you (or bring to you). You will be surprised at how many of your Likes satisfy one of the 12 dependencies (refer to Chapter Six) or one of the 10 *natural* human desires which we will discuss in a later Lesson.

A Player must always be aware of his or her "general personal values". General personal values (based off your Likes and Dislikes) help you make easy decisions. If you are in a situation or environment that is against your general personal values and Standards (which you'll discover in phase three) then you leave. When you choose to stay in a situation or environment that goes against your general personal values and Standards then you are in violation of the Game. Why? Because you are acting in direct opposition to who and what you truly are and that is not being responsible. A lion doesn't play and run around with zebras, it goes against his very nature.

Remember a King doesn't wield much power outside of his kingdom. This kingdom we're talking about is both physical *and* mental. A king rules from his castle; he remains in situations and environments he enjoys and wields power in. He only leaves his kingdom to expand his kingdom. Whether the king meets with other kings to discuss political matters or he needs to lead his men during war the king is always focused on his kingdom.

You should always be moving toward your Likes and away from your Dislikes. **Not running from them** (because that is fear) – but keeping them at a distance from your castle gates. You can't control everything, but you almost always have a choice.

When you're ready it's time for the third and final phase.

Phase Three: Standards (Core Personal Values)

When you get another quiet moment to yourself you can go over your answers from phase two and begin to pull out your Standards. Again, sometimes these are called your **core** (essential) personal values.

What are you looking for exactly? You are breaking apart your answers and simplifying them down to their very **core**. This process should give you *one single word*. That's right, get some more paper and grab a dictionary and/or thesaurus if you need them. You need to understand fully, the words you will choose to use. If anyone ever questions you about your Standards (and you choose to answer them), you will be able to explain yourself with unshakable confidence.

A simple example. Let's say one of your Likes was money. Then after you asked the question, "What benefit do I get from this?" You came up with a long list of what money can buy you. Your list might also include how much freedom it can bring – You can come and go as you please, travel and see the world. Also on that list might have been the ability to help people in need. When you get down to the **core** of these two answers, you can see two possible Standards emerge:

(1) Freedom
(2) Philanthropy

(1) You desire to be able to buy what you want, when you want and be able to go where you want, when you want. (2) You also want to add to people's lives, whether materially or socially.

As you go through all your answers you will see many themes that relate to one another. The single words you come up with will often repeat themselves over and over again. These are what are referred to as your **core** personal values. In the Game they are called your Standards. These are what you need to "stand on" as a Player at all times, no exceptions.

Knowing your Standards (**core** personal values) has four main benefits:

(1) It will further develop your character and integrity (we'll cover these in detail in a later Lesson).

(2) Knowing what you value most (and standing on it) will increase your value to others.

(3) Many of your fears and anxieties about life will fall away because you will have a deeper understanding of yourself.

(4) You will develop a sense of inner strength that will be felt by those around you. This is the beginning stages of your "Player's aura". An energy generated by you that others will "feel" and "sense".

There are more benefits but these are the ones you will probably notice first.

Knowing your Standards are one thing, living them is yet another price that must be paid to develop yourself into a Boss Player. Let nothing and no one turn you against your own Standards (**core** personal values). You are responsible for what you know and knowing yourself is the greatest responsibility of all.

As you learn to live through your Standards and the knowledge of the Game you will begin to define your purpose. Some people believe discovering your purpose is a dramatic moment – the skies will part, the world will slow down and trumpets will blow. This is not the case. You will however feel a surge of energy and a feeling of excitement will come over you. It will feel *right* for you. When that time comes do not hesitate. Write it down or record it somehow, you do not want to lose that thought!

A purpose is something that you should be willing to die for. It is the ultimate form of commitment. A purpose should make you feel a deep sense of satisfaction when you define it. It is tucked away, hidden in plain sight inside your Standards (**core** personal values), Likes and Dislikes. A **clear** purpose should answer three questions at once:

What should you become?
What should you do?
What should you have?

Peep Game – This is order: You must **become** first. This all starts with you and the Principle of Reciprocation (giving to receive). Once you **become** first, then you know what you must **do** in order to earn the right to **have** what it is you want. This is your own personal trinity.

Peep Game – This is confusion: Squares get this backwards; they try to **do** things first, so they can **have** things, so they can feel like they've **become** something of value. This is what they've been conditioned to believe.

Being of value is not based on what you have; it's who you are regardless of whether you have anything or not.

Now you know better.

You never need to explain to anyone why your purpose feels right for you. Most Squares wouldn't understand anyway. They are led by their desires and spend their lives feeding their emotions and because of that they are never satisfied and will find no rest. This why I called their way confusion in the paragraph above.

A Player is also never satisfied but for a different reason, they have a mission in life and will do whatever it takes to accomplish it.

The shortest distance between two points is a straight line but that line may not be the best route to take. There may be obstacles in the way, things you might have to climb over or move out of the way. Sometimes its better just to go around, that's the circle; the movement of a Player. They don't change directions, they just go around.

A Square on the other hand "bends a corner" or "turns a corner" when they run into any obstacle. They don't try to go around the obstacle they just end up going a different direction entirely. This is one reason why they never end up anywhere.

Going back to the structure of the Game (the pyramid), once you define your purpose you elevate yourself to the top of the pyramid. From that height you can see things clearer and you can see the roles of those below you. As they work and struggle to find a happiness that doesn't exist, you sit in contentment knowing that your life is no longer a mystery. Your life becomes something of meaning. No more worrying, no more guessing, no more wandering aimlessly in the dark. Every word you speak, every thought you think and every action you take starts beneficial cycles of Justice that allow you continually evolve in a pre-determined direction. The direction you chose for yourself. This is self-empowerment and its highest level.

LESSON 2: Self-Confidence (Breaking Yourself Apart)
According to the dictionary confidence means:

(1) *A feeling or consciousness of one's powers or of reliance on one's circumstances – Faith or belief that one will act in a right, proper, or effective way.*
(2) *The quality or state of being certain.*

If you went online right now and did a search in a search engine about self-confidence you would get hundreds of different definitions and a hundred of different ways to improve it. No one has a clear answer because people can't really define what self-confidence is. They don't have Game. We'll forgive them for that.

The reason for the confusion is because self-confidence is **not** the *gaining* of something; it is the *loss* of something.

What are we losing, you ask? We are losing, or I should say letting go, of everything that is not for us anymore. Every quality, image, lie and fantasy we've been taught and accepted in our lifetime. We are letting go of any and everything that will take us away from our purpose and weaken our Game. To sum all this up simply, we are over-ruling (overwriting) mental patterns that are no longer good for us.

People lie all the time and say they don't care about what other people think of them. I say, "Yes you do."

That's why you dress a certain way. You dress like people in your social circle, however small. That's why you eat what you do; you eat foods that are acceptable by your culture. If I went to an American restaurant and asked for a dish of monkey brains they would call me a lunatic. But in certain parts of the world monkey brains are considered a delicacy.

As human beings we have **natural desires**. These are desires that were *not* given to us; they are ingrained in our DNA, our genetic make-up. One of these natural desires is to be accepted by our social circle. Human beings were created to work together. We were created to function in tribes and families. This is a reality. In the Game we recognize this and accept this. This is why investing in people is so powerful. It speaks to our natural human desires.

You want to know what self-confidence is? It is accepting the fact that we want to be liked, admired and respected for our opinions. It is accepting the fact that human beings have a natural desire to feel as though they are in control of their own fate.

Confidence is being certain in everything you do, say and think. Even when you are *not* certain, taking responsibility for these things will make you *appear* confident. Peep Game. You must learn to be more direct instead of indirect. This requires breaking your social conditioning.

The Game gives you confidence because you learn to accept our natural human desires and feel no shame about them. We learn to value what we think of ourselves over what others think of us. We care what others think of us, just not as much as we care about what we think of ourselves. We care about other's thoughts and opinions, but not as much as we care about our own thoughts and opinions. Is that too much to swallow?

If you told this to people, many of them would call you selfish and arrogant for thinking this way. But if you asked those same people are they genuinely happy in their life, they would lie and say yes when they know they're not. Why do they lie? Because they care what *you* think about them! They don't want to seem like a bad person. Peep Game.

I can walk into a room of a hundred people and only maybe one or two of those people will be sincerely, genuinely happy. Why? Because happiness is an effect. Every effect must have a cause. What is the cause? The reality is you are only **happy** when things are **happening** your way. And another reality is, things almost *never* happen your way. That is a fantasy, it is a dream. It is something you must let go when you step into the Game. Don't forget that life is a series of problems that must be solved but this is what makes life worth living. It is through these trials and tribulations that we grow and we have the opportunity to strengthen our resolve and develop our character.

When you strip yourself of all the garbage that's piled on top of you, the real you that's underneath will shine through. This is what the Game does for you and that's the main reason people consider this information priceless.

You want to be more confident? Clear off the garbage that's on top of you. Drop it. Drop the baggage. Accept your past failures and mistakes and then drop them. If you cannot drop them, then you must over-rule them with a new mental pattern. Easier said than done but this is the price of making yourself into a person of value. This is the price you pay for strengthening your force. Working with yourself is the hardest work you will ever do. When you work on yourself, you will see your every weakness and have to find a way to correct it. No one likes to feel weak.

The benefit of this though, is that you will know yourself and you will realize that the qualities you honestly like and dislike about yourself, you see in others. What you see in other people is a mirror reflection of you. You can't truly see people for who and what they are because you are only seeing yourself. Sounds ridiculous? Let me prove it.

Look over your Dislikes list from Lesson 1. Now think about the qualities you dislike in other people, things that you hate and despise. You will see a connection. Do you want to know how deep the Game can get? I'll tell you. The only reason you see these negative qualities in other people is because they are *in* you. If they were not in you, you would never be able to recognize them in others.

Confidence is accepting your Dislikes. It is the brutal realization that our dislikes keep us in a state of fear and avoidance. We avoid things we dislike, everyone does. This is a natural human motivation. But now since you know your Dislikes and accept them you can move on and if you so choose, you can work on dropping the ones that seem foolish and over-ruling the limiting ones with a new mental pattern.

There is nothing wrong with having things you like and things you don't like. This is you, a reflection of the true you. The Game is always getting "you" back to *you*.

In Ancient Egypt they had mystery schools where they taught the secrets of life and existence. Before you passed through the first door you would read, "Know thyself," at the top of the doorway etched into the stone. The pyramid is the structure of the Game; "Know thyself," was the first realization a person should have on the path to enlightenment. Perhaps the Ancient Egyptians had a message for us after all?

Now let's come back to the word self-confidence.

Self – Your particular nature, personality and qualities. Being and accepting who you truly are (not what others have taught you to be).
Confidence – The state of being certain and the state of being conscious of one's own power.

Self-confidence is being conscious of your power and being certain in who and what you truly are.

Isn't that what the Game is about, self-empowerment? I hope this is even clearer now.

Here is a list of the 10 main **natural human desires**. Remember, these are desires that we have by nature, they were *not* given to us. People can (and do) work through these to manipulate and persuade. These desires must be learned and accepted for your personal growth and self-empowerment. This works because it helps you recognize leaks in your Game, areas where you are easily led or "give in" when it comes to wanting to fulfill these desires.

There is nothing wrong with these desires; they are a part of human nature. The problem comes when your entire life is based around one or more of these, you have a huge weakness in your character and therefore in your Game. Remember desire is tied in with emotions (Queen), a weaker force. You must learn to rule with your stronger force (King) and have a definite purpose (the gods or god – the only thing the King answers to).

(1) Be Accepted. The desire to be liked and respected by others.

(2) Be able to save money and/or make more money as well as save time.

(3) Feel romance. People want to feel love from sources other than family and friends.

(4) Be respected for their ideals. This is a form of admiration. People with strong ideals want those ideals to be heard and respected. This is especially true in their circle of family and friends.

(5) Have social contact. Most people have a deep seated fear of being completely alone.

(6) Have status. Yet another form of admiration, people desire to reach the heights of their own social group. These heights of status are dictated largely by their current environment.

(7) To feel secure and at peace. These words mean different things to different people but every person desires a feeling of security in their environment.

(8) Be able to determine their own fate. People desire to feel in control of their own lives as well as having the freedom to make their own choices.

(9) Eat. Getting food and water are the most basic survival instincts we have.

(10) Wield influence and power. No matter how buried this desire is, human beings want to be influential to others. Influence is a prerequisite to power.

LESSON 3: Integrity (Putting the Pieces Back Together)

There is no stronger person than an individual with integrity. Having integrity is not convenient and many times it is the hardest route to take.

Integrity is the quality of you; your very strength and originality in your nature. You are a Dominant Force, you are whole and undivided.

Integrity is a character trait that must be developed and perfected. It's like taking a rough diamond and cutting it little by little to the perfect cut that will give the best clarity. It is often times in us to want to do the right thing, but very seldom do we stand up and do it. But to truly have integrity you must be honest and have strong moral principles (Standards/core personal values). Knowing the Game and respecting the Game will bring this out of you. If you stand on your purpose and the seven principles you will develop integrity.

In our discussion of the seven principles of the Game the word intention was mentioned frequently. Intention and the principle of Justice go hand in hand. Your intention behind what you say, think or do is the measuring rod to what you can expect when your Justice comes back around to you.

Since you now are very familiar with the principle of Justice we can delve a little deeper into its aspects. Remember, Justice works off of everything you do, say and think. This means that you should always check yourself before you do, say or think anything.

In the Lesson on Concentration I will give you an exercise to help you get a better handle on your mind and thoughts but in this chapter we will be focusing on integrity – Meaning what you say and saying what you mean; saying what you will do and doing what you say. At all times no exceptions.

Your word is your bond.

Before you speak a thing to another person you must be aware of your intentions. Your intentions should be the measuring rod by which you say, or *won't* say something.

If you know you *don't* want to do something; don't say you will. When your word fails, you are showing weak character and damaging your reputation.

If you know that you *can't* do something; don't say you can. Your word will fail and once again this shows weak character and will damage your reputation.

If you know that you *can* do something but you cannot do it for another person when they want it done or how they want it done; don't say that you will. It's best to come to a compromise. You can also just say that you choose not to do it. There is no reason to lie. You admit you can do it, but *choose* not to. The other person may not want to hear it, but you were brutally honest and sincere. Because of this, that other person may not like what you've said, but they have little choice but to respect your character and integrity.

Lying shows a lack of integrity and weak character. The reality is, when you lie you are afraid of the other person's response. This is submissive force because fear is an emotion (Queen).

Never play yourself down to please another person.

Again this is putting you in a position of less value. There is nothing wrong with respecting or humbling yourself to people you choose to. Remember a King has little power outside of his Kingdom but that does not make him any less a King in his *own* kingdom. Just realize that there is a line between being humble and being submissive. There is a line between being helpful to another person and being used by them.

Never lie to please another person. Never lie to another person to avoid a response from them you don't want to hear. Never lie to avoid or create a situation you don't want to deal with. Well placed truths and well timed honesty are better than any lie. Silence can also be a powerful equalizer. Don't forget, a true Player always shows and takes responsibility.

You should never tell a truth with the **intention** of hurting another person's feelings (degrading their Queen). You should tell truths with grace, at the right time and placed properly. Your intentions behind what you say should not be malicious but should be said to educate, call attention to errors, mistakes and to uplift and inspire. This does not mean holding your tongue or acting with insincere niceness (playing yourself down). With mastery of the language most truths can be said with powerful impact without being bluntly rude. Being bluntly rude and bluntly honest are two different things.

Again, your **intention** behind what you say is the most important determining factor when you are gauging the return of your Justice. But you also want to be able to deliver when you choose to do something. Being able to deliver makes you a person of your word and improves your reputation. You become reliable and dependable to those around you. As I've said before, when your word is your bond you have the power to bring heaven or hell. When you say it, people will have no choice but to take it as truth because you will have a reputation of delivering. Many people equate this with gaining power through fear. You do not need people to fear you to gain power. Fear will move them away from you. People should not fear you but they should fear the *loss* of you.

Never judge or condemn a person on their mistakes. Judge them by how well they bounce back from their mistakes; how they recover, how fast they recover and get back on track. This is also how you should judge yourself. No human being is capable of never making a mistake. If the same mistake is repeated over and over however, that shows weak character. That person is either incapable or too lazy to see their mistakes and correct them.

Often time's human beings operate strictly on habit and you know these habits are nothing but mental patterns. People will act on these habits no matter how bad the Justice they receive from it will be. People act and talk the way they think. When a person knows better, they should want to do better. This is a person of strong character. But if a person knows better and does not want to do better, than this is a person of weak character. A person of weak character is a burden to others. They take little responsibility and have little (if any) self-reliance. They depend on others for their happiness, direction, resources and the fulfillment of their desires. This should never be you if you call yourself Playing the Game. You should be a self-contained unit but you cannot expect other Players and "Squares" to hold this perception. Everyone has free-will.

People in the Game use the term "Square" all the time. If you asked them what this means, they would tell you that a Square is anyone who is not a Player. A more modern definition is someone who holds a regular job. They don't have a design for their life, they live someone else's. They don't know the Game or they are misinformed about it. There is a deeper definition of the word Square. Let me explain this to you so when you call a person a Square, you know what you're really saying.

A circle is round and measures 360 degrees in circumference. A square has four points and each point measures 90 degrees. When you total up the four points of a square we get 360 degrees. Both the circle and square measure the same, but look entirely different.

Players should ALWAYS be Playing. They revolve around like a circle. They do not stop. Problems don't stop them, set-backs don't stop them, mistakes don't stop them and haters don't stop them. They keep it moving, they live life in motion.

Squares are the opposite. As they are moving through life when they face a problem, they stop and turn in a different direction just like the corner of an actual square shape. When they face set-backs, mistakes, people judging them, etc. they stop and turn a "corner", they go in a different direction. They never see anything through, they always change their minds. They may have a goal one week, and the next week they are focused on something different. What happened? They probably ran into a problem or someone or something bypassed their King (logic and reason) and influenced their Queen (emotion). Now they have a different goal.

A Square never accomplishes anything because they have no purpose. They never find rest because they are led by their desires which change day to day. Even if a Square has goals, they have weak character and no integrity so they Fold when things get rough. Things will always get rough at some point or another. Don't forget that life is a series of problems that must be solved. People of weak character either don't know or are too lazy to solve problems, so they don't. Squares always turn a corner and go in a different direction.

The circle and square both measure the same (360 degrees) but look different. A Player (circle) is not better than a Square because they are both human beings, they are similar but different at the same time. I'll say this again. You must learn to be a more direct Dominant Force. Leave indirectness to the Squares.

When you have Game, you have principles, rules, regulations and Standards you stand on at all costs. You must always, "Stand on it". Standing on the principles, rules and regulations of the Game is what gives you integrity and develops a strong character. Out of integrity and a strong character comes advancement (growth). Advancement and self-empowerment is a large part of what the Game is about.

Developing integrity and character are the formation of new mental patterns. It takes time, constant attention and consistency but you have that, right?

LESSON 4: Personal & Social Power (Examining the New You)

Wanting power and influence is a natural human desire. This desire is in each and every one of us to some degree, however small that flame may be. When a person seeks power they are seeking the right to control something – an event or another person. They are trying to produce an effect. Every effect comes from a cause. Without a cause there is no effect. So in order to wield power and gain influence you must know the causes. Knowing and using these causes will set the cycles of Justice in motion and bring you the effects.

The only person you should ever want total power over is yourself.

A word of warning, you should already know this but I'll repeat it again. Whenever you attempt to interfere with another human beings will-power you are setting a negative cycle of Justice in motion. You must ask yourself if you are prepared to deal with the consequences of your actions.

The best way to secure power and influence is by letting people give to you freely of their own willpower. They must take (not be forced to take) a subservient or submissive position to you. This is no different than you taking a subservient position to your boss at your job.

When you have Game, you possess knowledge that many consider priceless. We've only covered seven principles of the Game in this book and that is enough Game to empower yourself and empower a small organization of people if you so choose.

The Game is an anomaly; it is a mystery that people try to solve. When you are in the Game you take on the personification of this mystery. Your ways are foreign to the average Square but they cannot help but be drawn to you. They will "feel" your "aura" and be drawn to it. It's like how a moth is drawn to a flame.

A Square has been giving the perception (led to believe) that power comes from fear and respect. A seasoned Player knows that fear accomplishes nothing. Fear drives people away from you or makes them look for a way to undermine you. We don't want to push people away; we want to draw them in. Just like a moth to a flame. Respect from others comes naturally when you are respecting the Game. Respect is nothing that has to be forced when you Play a high level Game (Boss Player).

Said another way, when you have standards, principles, integrity and character, people will naturally "sense" that and respond to it.

When you have Game you are to keep Game. You never let anyone know what you're thinking. You reveal just enough to keep the mystery about yourself alive. When someone can predict how you think, they can predict your actions. When people can predict your actions, the mystery is gone. The flame loses its allure. A king always keeps a distance between himself and the commoners. The owner of a company rarely "hangs-out" with his employees. In this case you're keeping your plans away from those who don't need to know.

"The Game is to be sold, not told." The word "sold" in this rule of the Game doesn't necessarily mean money. People coming to you for Game (solutions to their life problems), knowledge, information, time, energy and/or resources, need to be "charged". Charging someone is what you require. Only you know what this fee should be. Your charging fee should be something that helps you in one of your goals or in your purpose. This is a fair exchange.

You can charge people by letting them grant you access to their resources, knowledge and information or by doing you favors. Again, this would be a fair exchange. Don't expect people to make the offer. You should ask for (not demand) your fee. And never feel "bad", ashamed or embarrassed to do so. This is being direct and being direct is wielding the stronger force.

Here is another way to look at the concept of charging. You can "test" a person's character and integrity. How? By testing their commitment to their *own* goals. You should only want to spend your time, energy and resources on people who are serious. If they are proven not to be serious, do not give them any more time, energy or resources than necessary – if any.

People who are serious will make an effort to keep their word. They will keep their word not only to you, but more importantly to *themselves*. This is one way to charge people. You "test" their commitment upfront before you develop your relationship any further. This is no different than getting a new job and being given a 60 or 90 day probationary period. Your employer wants to test your job performance and see if you're committed.

This is, **"cop and blow"** – to attain, and to allow to leave. You will have many people come into your circle and ask you for help and/or Game (cop) but only a small percentage of these people will stay around or prove to be of benefit to you. You must let go of people who waste your time, energy or resources (blow). In the Game, there are no contracts. People are free to leave or be dismissed at any time.

When respecting the Game, you never give priceless knowledge away for free. People must earn it. Just like you must earn the right to what you want in life, you must make others do the same. By doing this you are acting in accordance with the principle of Justice and the Game itself. Remember, the final choice must always be left up to them. You should not interfere with their free-will.

Why is the Game so alluring? Because it is outside of everything they have been taught about life. It is priceless information kept hidden. And even if you give Game to people, most people will still not appreciate what you gave them. The Game just isn't *in* them and that is perfectly acceptable.

The Game is a bag of valuable jewels and these jewels should not be given to just anyone. When you do not charge for your time, energy, resources or knowledge you diminish their value. Human beings place very little value on things they get free. Think about it. Family is free, your powerful mind is free, to a certain extent love is free and these things people place little value on. The reality is these things are some of the most important things in life. This is the sad state of human psychology but it is reality.

There was a study done of lottery winners who had won millions of dollars. It has been proven that over 70% of these big winners ended up broke within three years of getting that money. Why is that? That money was not earned, it was won. The money *is* rightfully theirs but they do not value it because they do not have the mental capacity and discipline to handle a sum of cash that large. They were ruled by their desires and destroyed by them.

Everyone wants more power and that includes you. You must recognize this reality and use it to your advantage. You must perfect the skills it takes to bypass a person's King and speak directly to their emotions (Queen). Do not forget, people's perception of the world is a fantasy. They like to think people are good and decent so they feel they also must behave good and decent. Meanwhile they are manipulated and used by those that have more power than themselves. This is why they were fed this fantasy to begin with. People with power have Game, and now so will you when you practice what's in this book.

Equality is another illusion. We are not all equal. Each of us has different strengths and weaknesses. This is not a bad thing; in fact it's a great thing. We are stronger together than we are individually. You must recognize your own strengths and weaknesses and be able to see them in others. When you ask someone to do something for you in an area they are weak in, you are setting yourself up for a Game leak. Would you ask a person who knows nothing about cars to give your car a tune-up? You should let people do what they are naturally strong at. You can help them work on their weaknesses, but remember this:

A person will perform best by doing what they want to do, what they like to do and what they feel confident in doing.

You must always be looking ahead with your mind focused on achieving your purpose. But you also need to look in your "rearview"; you need to learn from your mistakes and the mistakes of others. You are not a Square, you are a Player and you should be aware of what's in your circle (things you are responsible for) at all times.

At its core, power is the ability to make things appear a certain way – creating a cause for the desired effect. You must be able to give a fantasy and sell a dream but at the same time not be manipulative or deceitful. That sound impossible doesn't it? But it's not. All you have to do is develop the ability to share your vision (purpose) and the right people will be willing to help.

Remember the mystery and fascination of the Game? People will naturally be drawn to the warmth of your flame because you're in the Game. Your **intention** should never be to deceive and manipulate but to provide and place well-timed truths and honesty. Never ask anyone to do something that will put them in danger, harm them (or harm someone else). This is a major error; we call this "mismanagement". That's like asking a person who has never stolen a dime to go rob a bank. This is almost guaranteed failure.

Again, if you fully disclose *all* the risks involved and the person chooses to do it of their own free-will then that is their decision and their Justice. You will still reap the Justice of introducing the thought (idea) to them however, so Play responsibly. Your Justice will involve everything that grows out of the thought (idea) you introduced.

The average Square attempts to secure power through lies, trickery and deceit. They behave nice and decent but have a hidden agenda. When they come across anyone with real Game, they can no longer run Game and are forced to speak the truth. Lies, trickery and deceit are the "dark side" of the Game. Why not just speak the truth to begin with? What are they afraid of? They have limited Game (or no Game) and are afraid of not securing the power or advantages they desire.

You will be different because when you are a Boss Player (at the heights of the Game), you can run Game at such a level of proficiency that people will not even realize they have had Game ran on them. The winner is decided before the Game even begins. The Game is *in* you and what manifests from it comes completely natural.

Another weakness of human nature that a Square uses is justification. Trying to explain logically why they did something "bad" or illogical. Again, this is nothing but weakness. They are attempting to set up a situation where they are not looked at as "bad" or ignorant. The reality is they fear the response that honesty will bring them.

We have covered these few examples of weak Game to make sure you recognize this type of Game when you see it so that you can check it with your own Game. Game recognize Game. The strong overcomes the weak and the weak will try to raise its level.

It is not necessary to use lies, deceit and trickery to secure power. True power is secured be giving those without goals a goal. You can also give those without purpose a purpose. This goal or purpose should be in alignment with your own. But as always, you must disclose *everything* to them and they must agree of their own free-will. There is no worldly power without people. They are the cause and power is the end effect. Once you develop personal power, gaining worldly power is much easier.

What you're "selling" are your goals and purpose (vision) and those who are drawn to your flame will come help you in whatever capacity they feel they can. They desire something from you and you are getting something from them. If the **intention** is pure, the agreement is pure and the return of Justice will be positive. This is next-level (advanced) Game. Securing power through social means is the best way to secure power.

Now I must give you a bitter reality. It is another rule and regulation of the Game, and one of the hardest for a Player to ingrain in themselves.

Never completely trust anyone who doesn't have as much to lose as you – especially if things take a turn for the worst.

Having confidence in people is fine (believing they will do what they say they will do). Trust is not. Trust is submissive force. Trust makes you reliant on someone else instead of being self-reliant and responsible. You are never completely trusting of Squares. Why? Because you can never completely rely on people who don't *know* themselves. When a person doesn't know themselves they lack integrity and character. They have few standards and hardly ever abide by any principles. At the first sign of trouble they will either freeze up or turn and go in a different direction.

Remember, as a Player you have integrity and character (or are developing it) and the average Square doesn't. Reserving your trust for only those that have truly **earned** it by showing strong character and integrity is nothing but being responsible.

The Game is filled with disappointment if you have expectations. Keep your expectations in check and keep moving forward. You must learn to detach yourself from outcomes. The Game can be lonely but this is the price you must pay for the life you live.

As I've already said, the Game is seductive to those outside of it and although this draws people in, they have a hard time following the rules and regulations. The best expectation of a Square is not to expect anything from them at all. And when they do something, just ask that they do their best, give it their best effort because that is the best they can do. And when they give their best, acknowledge that, empower them and let them know that there has always been greatness inside of them. Also let them understand that they can push harder because there is always room for improvement. You should **know** this about yourself if you are in the Game. There is always room to strengthen and expand your Game.

Throughout everything remember to stay humble. Realize that you are never so high that you can't learn anything else. But you are never so low that you are completely lost.

Judge by results and how fast and effectively a person can recover from their mistakes. When you criticize someone, do it in **private**. When you praise someone, do it openly in front of others. This approach protects the ego and a person's Queen (emotions) and the praise fulfills one of our most basic human desires – admiration. This is especially effective on men.

The only thing you can ever know for sure is how *you're* playing the Game. You should always know where you're coming from and what you're willing to except. You can only be concerned with **your** Justice. Everything else is beyond your control, which includes when you invest in people. Things are not always going to go your way. People are not always going to "stand on it" and keep their word.

You will be let down but this should never stop you from Playing. You must constantly be Playing.

When you make predictions of future results, based off of Justice, never argue or try to force your point. That is an emotional response. Just say what must be said and let your point prove itself. When what you said manifests, your point will have proven itself. When you say it, people will doubt it. When they see it, they have little choice but to accept it. This strengthens your Game and requires very little energy from you. You never want to disperse your energy too thin, it weakens your force.

Just like a farmer plants seeds, waters them and makes sure they get enough sunlight, you must do this with people to secure your worldly power. Whatever seeds you plant in a person's mind needs attention and time from you so that they can grow. This book itself is many seeds and if you take these principles and knowledge you can water and grow a field for yourself. Do this for yourself *first* so you can show others. It takes a true Player to do that. This is why I don't tell you any of my life stories in this book. You must develop your own Game and please trust me when I say, it's not easy.

People with weak Kings (logic and reasoning faculties) are easily led. By learning how to use the Game you can raise a person's emotional state (or lower it). Play the Game right and lead people to be better and to be more than what they are now. They will become a testament to your Game and your Game will expand.

LESSON 5: Concentration (The Finishing Touch)
There are things you can do to help sharpen your most important tool. In the Game that tool is your mind. This is one of the keys to developing Dominate Force.

This exercise may seem strange to you and you may even feel silly doing it, but it will help you in everyday life. This exercise should be done every day for no less than 30 days. It is said a new habit takes 30 to 45 days to form. After the 30 days I would recommend doing it at least once every other day for the rest of your life if possible.

Concentration settles your mind and relaxes the body. With a settled mind and relaxed body your King rules over your Queen much easier. Your responses to events in your life will be much less emotional. You will also gain the ability to think clearer and better control your thoughts.

Don't forget, Game is not something you do, it is something that must be *in* you and then it must radiate (manifest) outward.

Concentration is defined as: *Complete attention; intense mental effort.*

It is through concentration that you will sharpen your mental faculties and be able to catch things that other people miss.

There is no such thing as multi-tasking. Your mind can only do **one** thing at a time. The more focused and concentrated the mind is on completing a task, the faster it will get done and with more accuracy. This is what you want. Everything you touch should shine with excellence, you should take pride in everything you do and everything you do should be the best you can do, every single time.

When you're multi-tasking, the attention of the mind is bouncing back and forth between two or more things. The energy is not concentrated, it is divided and therefore you turn your strong force, into a weaker force. Multi-task long enough and you will begin to miss small details. When you miss small details the overall task suffers and you actually slow down the speed at which it gets completed.

Concentration is concentrated force (effort) on one thing for an extended period of time.

The purpose of this exercise is to train your mind how to do this.

The benefits of concentration are numerous. With the ability to apply concentrated force you will far outshine the average person. You will be faster, complete more and make fewer mistakes.

(1) For this exercise you will need a quiet place to sit, preferably a place that is clean. You can sit on the floor or in a chair; you want to be comfortable. Make sure you don't have any tight clothes on that will be uncomfortable or restrict your breathing or movement. Put that cell phone on silent or turn it off and keep the children, house pet and other distractions out of the room.

When doing this exercise you are not to be intoxicated, under the influence of medication or narcotics.

(2) You will only need one object, it can be anything but it should sit at least three feet in front of you (no more than

five) and be at eye level. It could be a small plastic ball on a table or a small sculpture. It could be an ink pen that you stand straight up by sticking it into something, a small plant or even the flame of a candle (be careful that there is no breeze, we want the candle flame to remain as steady as possible).

The key point here is that this object must not be in motion, it must be placed in such a way that it will be perfectly still.

(3) Now sit and get comfortable and look at the object you just placed. You don't need to stare; it is fine to blink naturally. By letting your eyes close slightly, you can keep from straining. Relax with this and breathe normally.

(4) Now find one area on that object at look at it. It could be one letter or word written on the side of an ink pen, it could be the wick of a lit candle or it could be the reflection of light off an object.

As your eyes focus on that one specific area, you want to try to think of that and only that. It sounds easy but it's not. You will notice that your mind is rambling. You will notice thought after thought after thought. Your mind won't shut up! This is a divided unfocused mind – a mind of weak and submissive force.

(5) The goal is not to stop thinking and "clear" your mind, the goal here is to *ignore* what you're thinking and stay focused on what you are looking at. Do not struggle or get frustrated. Every time you notice your attention has slacked, check yourself and gently bring your attention back to the object. You may find yourself doing this multiple times a minute, this is normal; especially during your first few days.

What you're doing is training the mind to respond to you – to show it that when you want your attention on something, that's where it should be.

(6) Sit there is silence and make sure you are relaxed and comfortable. Being uncomfortable will break your concentration. If you feel your eyes watering up, do not wipe them unless you begin to feel pain.

(7) During the first week, hold this for two to three minutes a day. During the second week and all the way up to day 30 we want to be at no less than five minutes a day. And for day 31 and the rest of your life, no less than five minutes a day, every other day. You should challenge yourself and do 10 minutes from time to time when you have the time to spare.

Focused attention leads to concentration. So the act of continuing to focus your attention will train the mind to concentrate. Over time you will find that when you are working or trying to solve a problem, you can think clearer, even when you go to do everyday tasks like washing dishes, you will notice your mind does not wander as much. By the way, you can get in extra concentration practice just by focusing on things like brushing your teeth, bathing, and yes, even washing dishes. Bring your attention to each motion and feeling – ignoring the mind's random thoughts and concentrating on nothing else but the task at hand.

Concentration is the prerequisite to visualization and meditation, two arts that can be looked into if you so choose.

Concentration will increase the speed and power of your mind. It allows it to focus and reach out with effectiveness and will secure your self-empowerment. Learn this and most importantly, use it. Give it an honest try for at least 30 days and you will be surprised at the results. Once you've become skilled in concentration we can now use this skill to help us control our thoughts.

A Simple Thought Control Technique

This is a very simple process and like everything else in this book it requires practice and constant attention to detail. Since Justice operates from what you say, do as well as what you think, it is vitally important to learn to control the thoughts that swim around in your mind.

When we talk about controlling thoughts what we are really doing is cancelling and redirecting our mind away from destructive or self-limiting thoughts. I prefer the term "over-ruling".

Let's say you're driving on the road during an extremely bad rain storm. The thoughts of ending up in a car wreck may come across your mind. When this thought pops up we need to "blank" or "cancel" this thought out. This is not some form of visualization or positive thinking, it is simple thought control. We are learning to redirect our mind away from useless thoughts; thoughts that keep us constrained in fear and doubt.

When a thought like ending up in a car accident occurs, you much catch it **before** it yields you an emotional response. The Queen doesn't need to know a thing.

When you catch this thought say something to yourself similar to this, "I will not experience that reality." Or, "I over-rule that thought."

The exact wording is not important. What *is* important are that the words you use should move you emotionally. They should make you feel in control and powerful. You must find the wording that works best for you. The key here is that the words you choose should give a stronger emotional response than the destructive or limiting thoughts that you are trying to cancel and over-rule. This is a prime example of directing your King to instruct your Queen.

The concept is extremely simple, but catching the thoughts and using this technique takes a large degree of self-awareness. The concentration exercise in this chapter should have helped you in that area.

When slightly altered, this thought control technique can even assist you in breaking bad habits. You can over-rule the emotional and bodily cravings to do certain things. Again this takes a lot of determination, willpower and focus. New habits are formed in 30 to 45 days; breaking habits can take the same amount of time or more. Breaking bad habits is a true test of your powers of concentration. Be careful here, you cannot send your mind mixed messages. When you are trying to break a bad habit, just drop it. You cannot try to break bad habits while still indulging in them.

By using concentration and thought control you can cancel and override the thoughts that arise from your desire. What you are doing is breaking up the **mental pattern** in your mind that is the habit itself. You may even want to replace a bad habit with a new more beneficial habit by over-ruling it. This means that when the desire or thought comes up, you cancel that thought and immediately focus on something more positive or it's opposite. Conquer fear by cancelling the fearful thought out and think about being courageous. Stop eating bad food by cancelling the thought of eating a candy bar, then replacing that with the thought of eating a fruit or vegetable that you honestly like.

Denial is useless. It's a fantasy. You can lie to other people but you can't lie to yourself. Don't try to tell yourself you don't want something (or want to do something) because the reality is, you do. Instead drop it, cancel the thought and over-rule it with a better more positive mental pattern. This takes concentration and a lot of attention to what is going on in your mind but that's the price you must pay.

Please use some common sense. If you have an overwhelmingly destructive bad habit, you should seek the help of a professional. But for minor things that will build your character and help self-empower you, this technique can be extremely valuable.

CHAPTER TWELVE
Establishing Your Game & Some Final Words

Self-empowerment is all about winning. The average person will not try to win but they don't want to lose. A Player goes the extra mile because a Player wants to win; they play the Game to win. You should want everything you feel you deserve and you should feel you deserve everything.

Only a true student will be able to take the information and knowledge in this book and discover how to use it in their life. I cannot give you a road map or blueprint; you must earn the right to be a Player in the Game. I will however give you a few tips to point you in the right direction. What you're doing in the Game is designing *your* life – not being a part of someone else's design for your life. Let's start with some important words of wisdom. A reminder of the Game's greatest wisdom.

Before you can accomplish anything great in life, you have to know who you are *first*.

Once you know who you are, you can begin to establish your Game. Your Game should be structured like every system of power is structured. It should resemble the pyramid and you take the position of the capstone; the top of the pyramid itself.

When you know yourself, your first priority is to establish a purpose for your life. Once you have a purpose your next step is to establish your goals. Remember, all your goals should be in line with your purpose; they should be puzzle pieces that when all put together, form the image of your life vision. Once you have goals then you can develop a plan. This plan should get you to your purpose goal by goal, step-by-step. This creates order and structure in your Game. Order is Dominant Force.

Since you now know what you must *become*, what you must *do* and what you must *have*, you at this point become the king or queen of your own "kingdom". Or said another way, you are the owner/operator of your own "company". *You* incorporated. As king or queen, you become the highest level manager of your life. And as your life manager it is your duty to manager yourself – remaining a dominant force, remaining committed and staying focused on what you must do. You should be diligent in setting positive cycles of Justice in motion.

Your "kingdom" has positions. You, as king or queen, sit at the top of the structure and there are other positions open beneath you that can be filled (permanently or temporarily) by other people. If these people become members of your "kingdom" (company/team), by their own free will, it is your responsibility to manage them as well. They must completely know everything that is required of them and you should never hesitate to share your vision. You never reveal **all** your goals and plans because the mystery of you must remain. These people do however need to know your overall vision (purpose).

People respond to a vision more than they respond to ideas and plans.

Think of the most powerful people throughout history, they all had a clear vision (purpose). Ideas and plans may sound good, but a vision has value. Remember, value is one of the strongest motivators. The lower responds to the higher.

Over time you will help these people in your "kingdom" become empowered also. You should be willing to let them discover their life purpose and assist them is establishing goals – if they so choose. This sets a strong cycle of Justice in motion and this is in direct alignment with the principle of reciprocation. You are giving in order to receive. By empower others you become more empowered yourself. A kingdom of empowered people is much stronger than a kingdom (company/team) of only one empowered person. A king or queen needs hands and advisors, but it is the king or queen that always makes the final decision.

This is the most powerful way to expand your Game and get access to more and better resources. The more resources you have the more options you have in how and what to give. Many resources mean many options and opportunities. You should always take advantage of opportunities to expand your Game. You must be constantly Playing. Now let's move on to some final words and perspectives you should keep in mind.

First, you must learn to live life in fearlessness. Fear is a reality, it is an emotion. Courage is the opposite of fear. Courage is not the absence of fear, but it is continuing to move forward despite of fear. You must stand on it, you must stay in motion. Like I've just told you – know what you want, where you're going and make plans to get there. Step-by-step, goal by goal.

When you are in the process of *earning* something, it takes time. It will not happen overnight. Instant gratification is a fantasy. That desire is a weak mental pattern that comes from social conditioning. Trees do not grow over night, neither does grass. Babies take nine months to form in the womb and be born. Nature takes its time with things. It starts small and slowly grows over a designated time. Human beings think they can have things instantly and when it doesn't happen that first time or second time, they Fold and give up.

You will make mistakes. You must recover from your mistakes as quickly as possible and get back on course.

You will make bad decisions. By looking deeper into decisions before you make them, you can stop making so many bad (or destructive) decisions. Your decisions should be composed of a cause and the desired effect. When you truly understand the principle of Justice you can think about all the possible things that will grow out of your decision and predict the effect. If the effect looks like it will not produce what you want (or you are not willing to deal with it), then you must come up with a new cause, meaning you must think about making a different decision. To keep it simple, you must learn to look at all possible angles.

You must stay motivated. The root word of motivation is "move". If you are not moving, you are not motivated. You must constantly be Playing. This is what that means. If you lack motivation you need to find a better purpose for yourself. A Player is self motivated at all times. They don't need anything outside of them to get up and get moving day to day. A Player is a self-contained unit, responsible and self-reliant. This is may take some time to practice but once you develop this skill your Game will be that much tighter.

Your perspective on things is what runs your life. If you think something is bad for you, then to *you*, it is bad. If you think something is valuable, then to *you*, it is valuable. When you know your Likes and Dislikes you can see what your perceptions are. This gives you a base to change those Likes and Dislikes you feel are useless or limiting. Now that you know the Game, you should have new perspectives on just about everything. That's how powerful the Game is. You will "die" and be reborn into a stronger person full of integrity, character and Uncommon Sense. You will have a purpose, goals, principles and Standards (core personal values) that will make you a force to be reckoned with.

So now what are you going to do? Are you going to become a Player, or are you going to turn away from the Game? As the saying goes, you only get *one* chance. If the Game is *in* you, then even if you walk away, you will walk right smack back into the Game at some point. It may be a few days, months or even years but you will come across this information again somewhere else or even pick this book back up.

The Game is the ultimate mirror. When you look into it, you will see who you truly are. If you read this book and all you saw was nothing, then you honestly have very little ambition in life. Anyone who has even a little ambition to better their life will take something away from this book.

If all you saw in this book was how to manipulate people, then you are a manipulative person at heart.

If all you saw in this book was a way to impress people by sounding "deep" or "heavy", then you are a person of weak character. A Player never has to set a stage to look great. They are great because they need no stage. They shine all the time. Their very life is a testament to their Game. The average Square couldn't ignore them if they tried.

Since you now know this, when you are running Game or instructing people on the Game, you can also see *their* reflection in the mirror. They will see the reflection of who they truly are, and you will see their reflection too. Let me close this with a story. I don't remember where I got this story from, but I never forgot it so now I will give my version of it to you.

There was once a great King. He was loved by his entire kingdom. He ruled with justice and sound reasoning. His castle sat on top of a large hill and his subjects occupied the lands below.

One day a strange object fell from the sky into the river and tainted the water with a strange substance. This tainted water was used by the subjects of the kingdom to irrigate crops, drink and wash their clothes.

Over time the King started to notice that his subjects began to despise him, disrespect him and desired that he be removed from his throne. This hurt the King greatly because he truly loved his people. The King had met constantly with his advisors, the only people whom he could consult with and share his grief. They all agreed that the King should either step down before he was assassinated or give his royal knights the order to imprison and kill anyone that was found guilty of conspiracy.

The King thought long and hard about his decision and out of the love of his people he decided to concede his throne. He left his kingdom and became a mere Noble in another person's kingdom.

The moral of the story is that the King did not change. The King drank water from another water source that was never tainted and therefore he remained himself. The commoners on the other hand, drank tainted water and it changed their hearts and minds and they become unruly.

To the King, his people had changed. To the commoners of the land, the King had changed. It was all perception. Perception separated an honest King from his Kingdom. Perception can open and close doors. It can let people in and it can shut people out.

If you cannot get to the root causes of a person's perceptions, you cannot help them change themselves. And the ultimate reality is that if you cannot get to the root causes of your *own* perceptions, you cannot change yourself or empower yourself. A Player's perceptions should always be based on reality **not** "accepted" truths. Like the story above, hundreds of people can have the same perception; the same "accepted" truth and be 100% wrong. As a Player you will stand apart from the masses. You will be self-empowered and only be able to be understood by other Players. The burden is heavy but the rewards are tremendous. Peep Game. Now you must ask yourself, are you ready to play?

About the Author

W. James Dennis started his first business when he was 17 years old. It failed. He then started his second business in his early-twenties, which failed too. But just a few years later with an example of business success to learn from, his third business did succeed and he operated it for over 10 years. During this time he was a dedicated student of the "Game", something which he calls, *Uncommon Sense*. Realizing his passion was writing and educating, he changed gears in his life and is now an author, public speaker and small business consultant living just outside of Atlanta, Georgia – United States. His favorite quote is, "Keep it moving and keep it simple in the process."

Connect with W. James Dennis

www.wjamesd.com
wjamesdennis@gmail.com
facebook.com/wjamesd
twitter: @wjamesdennis

Also by This Author

Unlocking the Small Business Game – *The Playbook for Starting a Small Business from Nothing Using Simple Clear Uncommon Sense*
Holding Magnetic Conversations – *Learn to Be a Master Communicator in Just Hours*

www.ingramcontent.com/pod-product-compliance
Lightning Source LLC
LaVergne TN
LVHW051126080426
835510LV00018B/2264